Materials on Hand.

A poetic tale of compassionate caregiving

K. Page Nolker

D1361874

BABE EFFECT
www.babeeffect.com

Materials on Hand/K. Page Nolker
ISBN-13:978-0692911167
ISBN-10:0692911162
Babe Effect: 2017
kpagenolker.com

Cover design: artist-designer Anita Dore
Author portrait: artist-designer Matt Duquette

To my parents
for modeling love in sickness and in health.

"It's not what you look at
that matters,
it's what you see."
— Henry David Thoreau

Materials on Hand

I desired fulfilling love
And sought
My liberation
    A spiritual transformation
—I wanted something
More
Than everything
I'd known before.

I imagined my perfect lover
    Then conjured into being
Years
Spent caring
    For my mother—
Fucker!
That wasn't what I
Wanted
    To write an original tale
To find my voice—
The artist in me
    Set free.

I thought I'd paid my dues.
So this is how
The Universe
Pays me?
Obligated
To put my dreams
    And life
Aside
—Or so at first
It seemed.

Compassion
        And resentment
—Another test
The battle inside of me;
        Surrender and humility
If only they came easily—
Instead
They bring us to our knees
        Indifferent
To our woeful pleas.

But life is infinitely more
Than everything it seems,
And with its own creative schemes
        In time
It answers
All our dreams.

Fulfilling love?
I fell in Love
        With Life
—My cosmic lover
Not one
But everywhere
In everyone.

And of my art?
I came to understand
        The materials on hand
Are all we ever need
—The artist that resides within
Wants only to begin.

Foreword

When you turned ten in my family, my father made you a special wooden box with a lock on it. Made from materials on hand, no two were the same, but each came with the same message. A saying to live by: the Golden Rule.

On a yellow lined page of paper, my father wrote that if I looked closely I would see many imperfections in the workmanship, but I would know that a lot of love went into making my box. Human, my father was perfectly imperfect, like all of us, and yet to me he was an avatar. He embodied his humanity more fully than anyone I have ever known. *Materials on Hand* pays homage to my father and the standard he modeled as he cared for my mother at home over her six-and-a-half year decline.

My mother was diagnosed with Parkinson's and Lewy Body Dementia in February 2009. She was 76 years old; my father was 77. At the time of her diagnosis, my parents had been married for 52 years and living in Oxford, Maryland for 23. Prior to my mother's illness, my father joked that his role had been to read the junk mail and take out the garbage. An oversimplification, but not entirely untrue. During his career, my father travelled for work and my mother took care of everything related to raising the children and running the house; including the finances. As she became increasingly incapacitated, my father learned to shop, cook, clean, do laundry, pay bills—and serve as my mother's maid, bathing, dressing and even styling her hair. I was 43, divorced, and living in Buffalo, New York. The youngest of my parents' three

5

children, and the only one without children of my own, I assumed responsibility for supporting my father in the exhausting and challenging role as my mother's primary caregiver. When I was not physically with them at their home, I spent on average an hour every morning and an hour every evening joining them at mealtime on the iPad over FaceTime.

In the early days, shortly after my mother's diagnosis, my father shared with me the doctor's prognosis and advised that I enjoy my mother now while she still retained an awareness of herself. I remember the moment clearly, not because I shared his grief, but because I felt a terrible guilt—I loved my mother, but our relationship had never been what I considered enjoyable. Her love for me was unconditional, but her affection and approval were not. I spent years trying to decondition my defensive response to my mother; to not react. I mostly failed. Her dementia would be my ultimate test—there would be no more arguing; no more attempts to be understood. In the beginning, I found motivation through my loyalty to my father—the desire to return the love and generosity he'd unfailingly given me; to be worthy of his respect. As the situation continued to test me and demand ever more strength, I sought perspective in the Golden Rule and embraced my mother's care as a spiritual opportunity.

One afternoon, in the summer of 2014, at the beginning of what would be my mother's final year, I pulled out my journal and wrote a list of the many moods she cycled through in any given 24 hours. Watching her was tedious; the list was something to do. I titled that first poem, The Discord of Dementia, and posted it on Facebook. I had recently been to see the playwright Suzan-Lori Parks speak and been intrigued by her experience writing a play a day. I decided this would be a good exercise, and began to write one poem every day chronicling our events as they unfolded. Spending no more than 30 minutes, I dashed off the poems as a dialog with my mother; and in a style that mirrored the cadence of her fragmented speech. During my visits, my mother would ask, "Who's that tall girl in the kitchen?" Since she no longer comprehended our relationship as mother and daughter, she no longer understood that her husband was also my father. As a result, for clarity I mostly refer to my father as "your husband." As you'll read, even that relationship was not always clear to her, and both my father and I answered to any name. Rody, Jackie, Mary—Mother; these were the most common, and unrelated to anyone in her life at the time. Why those names? With the exception of Mother, that remains a mystery.

As days turned into weeks, then months, I developed a small, loyal following on Facebook and realized that sharing my experience was healing to more than just myself. For some, I provided a window into a day-to-day reality they couldn't imagine. Others, thanked me for giving a voice to their own caregiving journey. More than a few privately shared that they too had a difficult relationship with their mother and appreciated my self reflection as I worked to heal those wounds. Lastly, and not surprisingly, everyone fell in love with my father—responding to his extraordinary example of heroic compassion and his tireless good humor.

Though each poem captures a unique moment, themes repeat themselves as a reflection of the disease itself. Sleeping, eating, incontinence and bowel movements. Remembering and forgetting; restlessness, anxiety, delusions and hallucinations. Prescriptions, nutrition, exercise, doctors—and our desire for a non-medical death with dignity. On the surface, *Materials on Hand* serves as a primer on caregiving and dementia. As a whole—a timeless, archetypal love story with the kind of enduring romance universally longed for and seldom achieved. Read carefully, and you will recognize the stages of transcendence. The moment when resignation shifts to surrender and the experience as a whole assumes a different quality; becomes infused with an ineffable and transforming grace.

The roots of the Golden Rule trace back to a period in history known as the Axial Age, when in four distinct regions of the world, our current religious traditions began—all of them with the spirit of compassion as their core. The sages of the Axial Age were practical men searching for a solution to the aggression and suffering of their time. Living themselves amidst the violence and uncertainty, they concluded that it was not what we believed, but how we behaved that affected change. With an emphasis on attitude, they taught that by accepting suffering as an inescapable quality of human life, the experience could be used constructively to achieve a transcendent peace. If through self reflection and disciplined effort, we consistently cultivated the habit of caring and loved our neighbor as ourself with an open heart and practical support, we would, with time, experience an enhancement of our humanity—an altered state of being.

More than two thousand years later, we are still in need of the Golden Rule and a disciplined commitment to behaving with compassion, respect and universal concern for all humankind. We live in a period of history rife with fear and pain, not least of which is the trauma of disease and the burden of caregiving. Without knowing in advance that I was chronicling the same spiritual process that the Axial sages prescribed as a path to awakening, toward the end, I recognized the magic unfolding. Working with our own undesirable circumstances—the materials on hand—my father and I chose to practice joy and compassion and through doing so, opened to an inconceivable beauty and grace.

While he chose not to read my poetry, my father gave his consent to sharing our experience, aware that together we modeled an alternative perspective to the bleak expectation we'd been given. Honoring my promise to publish the collection, I offer *Materials on Hand* as a gift, that by sharing the love captured within this tale you too may find a way to transcend your own heartache and discover the potential for joy in even the darkest sorrow.

Notes to the Reader

This tale unfolds through a series of isolated moments. Though most are self explanatory, a few background details will help orient your experience.

Names: My parents are Richard and Lesley. My sister's name is Cary, and my mother's aides are a mother and daughter, Vickie and Vickie. Rody, Jackie, Mary, George are names my mother used, but do not refer to any actual people in this story. All of us answered to any name.

Vickie: In the fifth year of my mother's illness, we hired an aide, Vickie, to come in for 6 hours a day and relieve my father. Vickie came five days a week and her daughter, Vickie-Renee, covered most weekends. We could not have managed without their love and support.

Victor and Victoria: One afternoon, in the latter part of my mother's illness, she found and carried downstairs two baby dolls from the attic. Tucking them under a blanket, she made them comfortable on the couch, named them Victor and Victoria, and there they remained—real to her.

Jeanette: Though I don't call her by name, Jeanette was my neighbor in Buffalo whom I refer to as my second mother. Jeanette was 96 and recently widowed, when I offered to be one of her care companions. This involved walking next door to enjoy breakfast with her, or fixing her dinner a few days week whenever I was not in Maryland. Through this relationship I came to understand the intimacy of caregiving, and the process of letting go, from a different perspective.

Setting: My parents lived on Hel's Half Acre Road in Oxford, Maryland on Cemetery Cove. They built their home in 2005, but had lived in the community since 1987. A quintessential small town, friends and neighbors added greatly to the richness of our experience and their compassion and involvement made caring for my mother at home possible.

The Lake House: During the six-and-a-half years of my mother's decline, I commuted between my home in Buffalo and my parents' home in Oxford. The autumn before her death, I realized that my role as caregiver would not end with my mother's passing; that my father would continue to need my support. Tired of the long commute, I sold my home in Buffalo and moved into my family's lake house in the Pocono Mountains—a healing, magical place I knew my father would enjoy visiting.

Hallucinations: Hallucinations are a common characteristic of Lewy Body Dementia. For my mother, the experience ranged from mildly unsettling to frightening. We referred to her hallucinations as her "spirit people" and embraced them as though she had the gift of sight. Rather than denying their existence, we supported her in understanding that while real— and certainly they were to her—they were not material.

"No mud, No lotus."
— Thich Nhat Hanh

Premonition

Years before I ever wrote
—You knew I would.
You worried
One day
I'd write about you.

Third Person

On our walk today
We talked about Page.

You wondered if she is happy
—I assured you
I am.

A Single Mother Thanked Me

Seeing me
Out with you,
A single mother thanked me—
"One mother
Can care for five children;
But today,
Five children
Can't care for one mother."

Intense work
Important love
We outsource
The opportunity
    To grow

Familiar with death
For a minimum wage
To anonymous caregivers
Who may—
Or may not
—Care.

Only Love

I hold my mother
And weep.
She cries like a child.
She wants her mother
    She wants to go home.
Why won't I take her?
She is home.
I lift her
In and out
Of cars
And chairs;
Change soiled diapers
And bathe her.
Berated
For imagined wrongs
I smile
And say,
"I love you."
Remembered
Then forgotten—
I answer
To any name.
Restless
And distracted
We drift

From doing nothing
To doing nothing.
I practice patience
Learn acceptance
Experience peace.
Days creep
Full of nothing
And everything
    Only love
—Matters.

The Discord of Dementia

Endless days
The sum of moments
Mercurial—
Docile
Feisty
Frustrated
Sweet
Confused
Inconsolable
Tired
Agitated
Asleep
Busy
Still
Busy
Anxious
Distracted
Afraid
Delusional
Sarcastic

Stubborn
Incoherent
Innocent
Funny
Churlish
—Cherished.

The Art of Surrender

In the beginning
We nurtured hope
And courted denial
—Until we made space
for not knowing
And surrendered
What was
For what is
    Now
The endurance
Of enduring love.

One Poem a Day

I do not allow myself
To stockpile
Poems
Written in advance.
Instead,
I trust
One poem at a time
Along with you
Each day
New.

The Poetry of Dementia

She asks me for string
And I ask how much
—What is it for?
She needs it
She tells me
To tie up the evening star.

The Dao of Dementia

Through you
I finally found
—My Way.

A Tangled Mind

I hand you your toothbrush;
You brush your hair.

Love's Reflex

Your death does not worry me;
The details do.

You cannot void your bowels
Without help;
I cannot help
Without gagging.

Stamina

My father
Shares his new discovery
—The end of his tether
Is a loop.

Her World

My mother smiles at my father
Proud—
"The babies were so good tonight."

Phenomenal Woman

Light as a feather
Your skin ripples
In loose waves
Across your flat stomach.

Stiff as a board
I lift you
Into my arms
And you rise.

Death Comes

My father and I
Discuss dying
—Is it better to know?
Would you choose
To say goodbye—
One final hurrah?
Or slip out without a word?

He refers to quality time
        Remaining;
Laments that all the news
        Is bad.
Doctors, disease and deaths;
Friends suffering
Loved ones leaving
—A daily litany of woes.

I try to imagine
—And can't.

One loss overwhelms
The strongest among us;
So many at once—
A war waged
against life.

Company

Your friends came to dinner;
His mind is leaving
—Yours has left.

You introduce your hallucination
And he turns to me—
"We speak the same language."

A preview of the plot
For a script he did not choose
But graciously accepts.

Off the Cuff

*"You know—
I'm not as dumb as I think I am."*

Of course you're not dumb mom,
Where do you think I got my genes?

"The washing machine."

No Place Like Home

"Mother
  Mother!
Please!"

A mumbled recitation
Of unfamiliar names
Rody, Jackie, Dickie, Mary, Pat

"Please!"

The bus; the train; a ride
—Your daily refrain.
You long to go
To your childhood home.

Love's Touch

A synchronized effort
One
Undresses you
The other
Warms your gown.
We rub your feet
Every evening
—Ten minutes;
You begin to snore
In two.

Dramatics

Emotions
Exaggerated
 Were not tolerated.
But my mother
Is gone
And her child self
Is of a different mind
She likes to say—
"This is the worst day!"

Day after day.

If Memory Serves

You insist
You've eaten
What sits on your plate
Untouched.

Overheard; Again

"Darling
—Please
Just eat a few bites;
I won't mention it again."

"I've heard that before.
Three or four times.
—This month."

"You have a good memory."

"Yes I do."

Not Good

I wish you a good morning
And ask how you are.
You stare
Expressionless
Into the iPad
And without uttering a word
Raise your right hand
In a gesture of greeting—
    Pause
Then slowly arc your hand
Into a nosedive.
You stare
Expressionless
Into the distance.

Questions and Answers

"Mom
—Where are you going?"

"Downhill."

Do You Know the Way?

Hel's Half Acre
—The road you live on—
Runs straight
From the mailboxes
Through the soy field
To the stop sign.
We walk three times a day
And every day
You want to know—
"Is it okay?
Do you know the way?"

Anxious

Fire
Theft
Sightings
And missed appointments—
Fictions
And hallucinations;
The worrisome world
Of a missing mind.

Dire Non-Sequiturs

Imploring;
Tears.

"Don't you understand!??
I have no place to put the boats this afternoon."

A Proper Woman Does Not Curse

A proper woman
does not curse;
Does not say damn
Or anything worse.

There was sugar for shit
And crud for crap;
God was forbidden,
We'd be given the strap.

But times have changed
Your mind rearranged,
And in a moment quite blunt
You called me a cunt.

Mother's Day

You were the opposition
To my disposition;
You gave me struggle
    And strife—
You gave me
My Life.

The Morning Report

Every morning
I ask how your night was—
A few are: Good
Others are: Fine

A sarcastic: Fantastic!
Is my father's standard line.

"Your mother was ripshit"
—That's a whole different class.

Sleepless and mean
It's not a good scene.

Two Sides of the Same Day

A.M.—
Your husband
Sends you into the bathroom
At Walmart
Alone
And waits
    —A long time.
When you come out
You hand him your turd.

P.M—
You lecture him.
*"I don't like
Being treated
Like a little girl.
You don't know
What it's like
—It's pretty crappy."*

Pissed

Vigilance
And cranberry juice
Are not enough;
    Infections come
—You come undone.

The Rearranger

Balance
And color
—The aesthetics
Of composing
Nuance;
A feel
For arranging
Beauty
—I learned this from you.

So will I one day
Be like you?
Moving this here,
Hiding that there.
At it all day,
You still rearrange.
Only what once
Was an art
Has now become
—Strange.

Without Haste

Sustained
In this state
Of suspended
Reality
By your disordered
State
Of Grace
—We know
No haste.

The Lucid Moments are Hardest to Bear

"Darling,
Don't cry.
It's not your fault."

*"You have no idea
What it feels like."*

"I know—
There's nothing fun
About what we're going through.
It's no fun for anyone,
But we're here
And we're making the best of it."

*"I know—
I feel sorry for you."*

Cover Wars

She pulls the covers
    He pulls back.
She insists
It's time to get up;
He holds her
    Down.
Caresses
And coaxes.
She fusses
And fidgets.
Their day begins
    In the dead of night.

Home; Again

"I want to go home
—Just one time
I want to go home.
I want to visit my mother
I haven't seen her in years.
I miss her so much.
Can I go?
—Please?
Just one little time."

"Darling,
We are home.
This is our house;
These are our things."

"You have a thousand excuses
Why

I can never go home.
I want to see my mother!"

"Darling,
Your mother is in heaven."

"No!
Any excuse
Is an excuse."

Dream Weave

In my dream
I am flying
On a jet plane.
The engines have failed;
The pilot asks us
To take our seats.
I feel calm
    —I am lucid;
Surrendered
To a fate
Which never arrives.
Instead,
The pilot lands the plane;
I shake his hand
—And wake up.

You were awake
While I was dreaming
    —Insistent
You had a flight
You needed to catch.

The night before
—In my dreams
I went to school;
Restless and awake
—You wanted
To go to school.

Miles apart
In different states
Where is this place
Our minds meet?
What is this shared space
I visit in the night
That you confuse with day?

Respectfully Wrong

You complain—
We treat you like a child;
We're always telling you
What to do.
You're always wrong
     —That's right.

We try to respect
     Redirect
Not correct
You,
But still—
We're forever saying
No.
No.
No.

How does it feel?
—How could I know?

Another One of Those Nights

Your husband wakes
To your weak punches.
A vision—
You've fastened his belt
Around your gown;
Are wearing his shoes.
You have brought him the phonebook
    Panicked
The house is on fire.
He needs
To call the fire department
    Now!
You bang on the walls
And yell—
"Help!"

Talking to Strangers

I stand back
And watch you
Talk to strangers
—Something you have always done.
You are still funny
Charming
And kind;
Your audience
Erupts
With laughter.

But others
Turn to me
Eyes wide
—Lost
In your world.
They fear you—
As if your non-sense
Will ensnare
their own minds.

Accustomed
To order,
They lack
Your rules
Of engagement—
They do not know
How to be
With a mind
That's free.

The Word is Any

You corrected
Vickie's grammar
—She and I
Burst out laughing.

Your aide
Vickie
Fits like a third daughter.
Embraced
By us
As family;
She's treated

Like family
By you.

Bathroom Humor

Had roles been reversed
    And it was my father
Not you—
I try to imagine
You
Calling me
To share
The truly gross
And horrifying;
Or the way we laugh
Until we're crying.

Hallucinations and Intrigue

My father
Leaves the room;
You look at me
And whisper—
"What did you mean
When you said
You have to watch that guy
—He has a lot of hair?"

"Intriguing mom,
But I don't know.

Could it be
Your spirit people talking?"

—I ask you.

You answer—
"I guess so."

And then you want to know—
"How do I tell?"

Your Basic Needs

The cover wars
Began at two
—You'd won
By five.
Dressed
And set free
To wander
Outside
Carrying
A lampshade
Filled
      With important things—
Two
hand towels;
A roll
Of paper towels.
Your husband's
Cell phone;
An empty pocketbook.
—The things you took.

Chew on This

Dinner
Does not appeal
To you
—But eating
Your paper napkin
Does.

Your Attention Please

If you felt
Unheard
Marginalized
Invisible
—As I know
Sometimes
You did—
How do you feel
Now?
Indisputably
The core
Of our world
—The focus
Of everyone's
Every
Day.

As You See It

Over the iPad
Your husband
Gives me

The rundown
On last night.

You roll your eyes
And interrupt—
*"Dick,
You really are
The king of charm:
I, I, I, I, I
—I did this
And I did that."*

Out of the Blue

*"Are you trying
To tell us
You're pregnant?"*

"No.
Definitely not.
I don't think I can
Get pregnant
Mom."

*"Oh.
That's a nice feeling."*

And I'm left
To wonder—
I arrived
Out of the blue,
Was I not
A nice feeling,
Too?

Whatever Works

Your guard down,
I slip your pill
In—
You spit it
Out.
Lips pursed
In stubborn refusal.

I've watched
Your husband
—At a loss
And afraid
    Of losing
His patience—
Silently
Leave the room.

He takes a moment
To collect himself
And when he returns
    You cry—
Upset
For upsetting
Him.
You take your pill.

So I try this
As a strategy
Of desperation
Once
An hour of patience
And pleading
Have failed.

Without a word
I leave the room—
Exaggerate the sound
Of my steps
        —And wait.

When I return
You take your pill
And eat.

Every evening
Is a struggle
Without sense
In an engagement
Of endurance.

Practice

Without warning
You freeze.
Still
As a statue.
Motionless
And unresponsive.

"Hello?
Mom?
Are you there?"

You do not acknowledge
Me;
Will not respond.
Your eyes open
Are vacant.

I wait.

Eventually
You return
To this world;
But each time
I am reminded
That someday

—You won't.

Grace

We took our after-dinner walk
Last night
And at the top of the lane,
Once we'd turned to head
Home,
You stopped—
"I forgot to say my prayers."

You stretched your arms out wide—
"Let us hold hands."

Together we stood
In the middle of the lane,
The dog and cat
As congregation,
And spoke the Lord's Prayer.

Your husband began
The twenty-third psalm.

I followed with
Amazing Grace.

Swing Low
Sweet Chariot
—Delivered us home.

Up in Smoke

My cannabutter
Bombed.
I wanted to give you
An appetite;
I wanted to give you
Tranquility.
Your worry
Worries me
More than the law.

Some Things Never Change

We mentioned
Last night
About a party
Tonight.

You woke in the morning
Anxious and worried
—About what you'll wear.

Love Wins

Your good friends gathered
For the Preakness
And in a five dollar pool
You drew the winning horse.
They cheered
And clapped
For you;
Shouted—
"Yay, Lesley!
You're the winner!
You won!"
And although
You didn't understand,
You beamed like a child
Lit up and happy
—Victorious
With love.

Memories Unmoored

My father and I
Went sailing.
We left you
    And our worries
On shore
—Sailed away.

But the smell
Below deck
Summoned memory
And there before me

—Younger and smiling,
I saw you.

Mary is Contrary

Agitated—
Your eyes closed
—You mumble
Your daily litany
Of names.
At Mary
I interject—
"Mary, Mary
Quite contrary?"
Without missing
A beat,
Or opening
Your eyes,
You reply—
"Yes.
With cockle shells
And silver bells.
Mary, Mary
That's contrary

—Please!"

Gratitude

"Sweetheart,
How 'bout giving me
A smile?"

*"I'd rather give you
A kick in the balls."*

Love

Self-love
—The hardest
Love of all.

I say
I love you mom
And you reply—
*"I know.
I don't know why."*

Each time
You say this
I want to cry.

Our Weekend Away

You helped
Your husband pack
　　—Art off the walls
You made ready to go,
The things you might need
You just never know.

Candlesticks
Rocks
And kitchen utensils,
Tucked in with
The clothes he chose.

Distracted
    By taking stuff out—
The essentials
We travelled without.

One Love

Loving you
Is a group effort—
I relieve my father;
My sister
Relieves me.

She and I
Discuss death
    And life
In hushed tones
As you lay sleeping.

When you wake
She comforts you,
And watching her
—I see myself.

Bittersweet

Tomorrow
I leave
For Buffalo
And leave
—You.

My body
Mind
And spirit
Will welcome
The break.

A respite
You
And your husband
    Will not get

Until the end.

No Sense

Your dentist
Wants to schedule
A complicated
Invasive procedure
To remove
A tiny cavity
Beneath a crown.
You cannot sit still
For a half-hour cleaning
Or keep your mouth open
    Unassisted.

You do not
Brush your teeth well
—You cannot
Be made to.

Most days
We hand you
Your toothbrush
     —You brush your hair.
We try to help;
You clench your teeth
And scowl.

Are your teeth
That important
—When you do not eat?
Does the dentist not see?
Is it a lack
Of common sense?
     Or common decency?
I am tempted to be incensed
—But know well enough
There is no sense
In that.

The Caregiver's Litany

A UTI
And a stye
Under my right eye;
A cold sore
And a throat that's sore.

Last Words

I helped you
Into the car
    Said I love you
And said goodbye.

You smiled
And replied—
"Goodbye dear.
You really are a neat kid."

Love Remembers

"Hello Page.
I really missed you today.
I kept looking for you."

Point of View

You tell your aide Vickie
You want a cinnamon bun.
She agrees to buy you one
If you agree
—To eat it.
You say you will.

She drives you
To Dunkin' Donuts
Pulls up to the drive-thru
And rolls down the window.
From the passenger seat,
You lean across her body

And yell—
"HELP!"

Flashing the young man
Behind the window
A calm smile
Vickie hands you the bag
While she pays.

You pull out the bun
    Then throw it at her.
She puts it back in the bag;
You pull it out again
—And eat it.

Still smiling,
Vickie turns
To the stunned young man—
"Makes your job look pretty good
Doesn't it?"

Not Fooled

Since you no longer
Remember
What to think,
It's tempting
To tell you
What you
—Should think.
But while you
May be out of sync
You are still
A step ahead,

And when your husband
Tells you—
"This is your place
Where we live
And where you
—Are in love with me."
You reply
To no one in particular—
"He's directing me again."

Where We Meet

In my garden today
I felt you
And how very much
Alike
We are.

Hooky

I didn't write you
Yesterday;
I left for the beach
At eight—
Your poem could wait.

Dress Rehearsal

It is not enough
To let go
Of you,
I must release
Your surrogate, too.
I am a childless mother
With two mothers—
Both of you
In need
Of maternal comfort
And care.
Like a synchronized fate
My neighbor and friend
Has chosen now

To die
At home
With comfort care
Around the clock
Including me.
A dress rehearsal—
I love her
As I love you.
Honored and calm
I feel anxious, too;
Afraid of breaking down
—Overwhelmed
By letting go
Of both of you.

Happy Meal

Two French fries;
One bite of turkey.

"Dick,
I've had a good meal;
I've had a nice happiness.
I couldn't possibly
Eat any more."

Good Advice

"Why don't you all stop
Trying to figure me out.
Just lean back
—And enjoy it."

Sly

You turned
—Eyes looking directly
Into the iPad
    At me
You winked.

"I saw that."

You smiled,
Ever so slightly
—And nodded.

Peonies

I used to rush
Fading flowers
To the compost.

Caring for you
I've come to see
The beauty
In decay.

Comfort Never Was Your Gift

Your husband invites you
To join him on the iPad—
"Come cheer up Page the Rage;

She's had a hard day.
Tell her everything is going to be okay."

"It probably isn't."

Pantry Poetry

I cleaned
And rearranged
Yesterday.
Wrote poetry
    In form—
Lines of glasses
And stacks of plates;
Punctuated space
With objects of grace.
I took off doors
The better to adore
These things
We share;
This history
We bear.

Rearranging my View of You

I placed your dishes
In my pantry;
Rearranged my minimalist view
To accommodate a larger
    Appreciation of you—
And your treasure line of ancestry
The details of your history.

Crystal, linen and lace;
These things are not my taste.
Silver, porcelain and brass;
Symbols of comportment and class.
Like my preference for black
And white
    —We are as different as day and night.
Your silver and dishes in pink
These things are now our link.

Feral

Where is the rage
In Page?
It is not
That anger
Was not
Tolerated—
It simply
Did not
Exist.

Was not
Acknowledged
—Never modeled.
No passionate
Arguments
Raised voices
Or fits.

Only humor
And strength
—Volumes
Of silence.

This I learned
From you
Who now
Unfiltered
Unrestrained
Bear your teeth
And growl.

Visceral
And effective
—I'd like
To do that too.

At the End of My Tether There's Love

I asked your husband
About his day
—"Great!"
Was his reply.

What made it
Superlative?
I need to know why.

"Just being here
With your mother;
Just being alive."

Too Late

It was one of those nights;
So when you ask
For a push

Your husband asks you
"What for?"

"So I can get up."

He gives you a nudge
But no more.

"I need a bigger push."

He offers you a pull—
Into his arms.

*"If you don't hurry up
I'm going to poop
In my pants."*

He springs into action—

"Too Late."

No Variety

Your husband tries
To cook
What you'll find pleasing.
A new skill
Acquired for you.
Last night
He made crab cakes
And succotash.
You closed your eyes
    Indifferent
—Immune to his appeals.

"Please
One bite;
I try to make things you like."

Inspired cuisine
—A taxing routine.

*"Dick,
I am rather tired
Of listening to you."*

And so it goes
Night after night.

Trust

Another uneaten meal
—Your husband turns
The iPad
So that I see him;
See the worry in his face.

"I'm at the end of my wits;
I don't know what to do."

I pause
—Heartbroken
I'm not there in person
When I say—
"Maybe it's time."

Time to trust
That your spirit
   —Your soul
Knows
—That it's time.

Lighter Fare

There's also the fact
That the cook
Is a novice.

"How do you like
The shrimp and grits?"
—He asks.

"Do you really expect me
To tell you the truth?
—They're not that good."

"Well, let me ask again
And I'll tell you what
I want to hear—
Tell me they're terrific!"

Big News

You woke your husband
In the middle of the night
With a loud and urgent—
"Mother! Mother!
—I think I'm pregnant!"

Your husband assured you
You aren't;
You answered—
"I may be."

Was it Rody, Dickie or Jackie?
—That's what I want to know.

I Really Love You

In a tender moment
Of spontaneous emotion
You turn to your husband
And share—
*"I really love you
I love you so much."*

"I love you too sweetheart.
To love
And be loved in return
Is the nicest thing in the world."

You agree;
Then add to your list—
"I love Mrs. RTN"

—That's you—

"And two other people, too."

By The Numbers

I want to tell him
    No more
Blood pressure
Charts;
And daily weigh-ins.
No more counting days
By the hours.

My father
In a wrenching moment
Laments—
"I was told things would
Progress
And apparently
That's true."

I want to tell him
Let's love
What is—
Remaining;

Let now—
Be enough.

Let now—
Be everything.

I want to share
Her words:
My poem
Good Advice—

"Why don't you all stop
Trying to figure me out.
—Just lean back
And enjoy it."

Reaping

Peace and love
Goodwill toward friends
It is these things
That matter in the end.

Humbled by gratitude
It is your lifelong attitude
That brings so many to your door
Offering always to do more.

Meals on Wheels

They come calling
Bringing food and love;
Invitations and support.
They fill your refrigerator and pantry
With dinners and pastries.
Week after week
Months pass into years.
So many friends
For whom you'd do the same.
A community that cares
Makes even this
Much easier to bear.

Empty Calories

I watch you
Through the iPad
Decline to eat
Your dinner.
What should I feel
When I watch you
Choose instead
Your paper napkin
For your meal?
Ripping bits
You fill your mouth
And chew.
This is not new
And still
I cannot comprehend
—Nor through the iPad
Convince your will to bend.

In Sickness as in Health

Your husband called
After putting you to bed;
He wanted to report
All the thoughts
Running through his head.

For the second time
    Three years apart
A good friend
Sought to bring an end
To this love so true,
He does not comprehend.

He tells you
It's for the best
—Your wife belongs
In a nursing home—
You need the rest.

He cannot imagine
Doing what you do
—You cannot imagine
Anything more true.

Still Crazy After All these Years

"Sugarplum
—You ready to take our dessert walk?"

A Gripping Mood

You have been
These past days
In a gripping mood.
Grasping
And growling;
Clenching
And crying.
No coaxing
Or prying
Changes your mind.
Objects of your desire
You seize
Without tire.

You Again

Every morning
The bells on the backdoor
Ring
When Vickie arrives
And your husband
Announces joyfully—
"Heeeere comes Vickie!"

An angel of compassion,
She enters the kitchen
With a huge, radiant smile
And a warm hello.
She brings you treats
And greets you first.

This morning
You're not in the mood;
Your greeting is rude—
"You again!?
You're always following me around.
How long are you going to stay?"

Virtual Reality

"Page,
Get back to the table
Right now!"

"Mom
I'm on the iPad
—I can't."

"That's too bad!
Get back to the table
Right now!"

Ignoring
her tone
—I wish I could.

Pot Calls Kettle Black

A friend
You see often
Gave your husband
A ride home from golf.
You walked up to the car
And asked—
"Who are you?"

When he gave you his name
You look surprised—
"The Lee from Oxford?"

He said he was.

"And who is that with you?"

He introduced you
To your husband.

When he pulled away
You turned to me
And declared—

*"I didn't even
Recognize him
—He's really aged!"*

Saucy!

You wouldn't
Undress
For bed,
So your husband
Decided
—Who cares!

What difference
Does it make
If you sleep
In your clothes
    —It makes
One less task
In the morning.

I asked
About your bra.
"We gave that up"
My father informs me—
"Her tits are gone.
They're little blueberries
Sitting on saucers."

How saucy!
My proper, wholesome
Mother.

Wife of a Preacher Man

Your husband
Does not go to church;
He goes
    Direct.
And every night
At dinner
He directs us—
To feel grateful.

"Lord, thank you
For all the wonderful blessings
Of this life.
Thank you
For this beautiful day
And for this food before us.
Lord, thank you
For our friends
And neighbors;
Thank you
For the fun we have
And the love we share.
Lord, continue to guide
And steer us
In All our endeavors
And we
Will be of good cheer
And make a joyful noise
Unto you."

And so we do.

Half Human; Half God

You
Vickie
And virtual me
Lingered
At the kitchen table
This morning.
Vickie and I
Sharing stories;
Exchanging news.

You were alert.
Your eyes tracked each of us;
Your facial expressions
Mirrored the conversation.
Occasionally,
You even chimed in.

And though the words
You strung together
Meant nothing,
You delivered your gibberish
With perfect inflection
    And timing.

You remind me
Of Anis Moijgani's
Spoken word—

"For the 2-year olds who cannot be understood
Because they speak half-English and half-God"

—Yes
This feels right.

Because I do not speak
This new language
You use,
Does not make it
    Less divine
—For surely you are.

Anis Mojgani; Shake the Dust

The Acme

Shopping
Has become
A group outing.
You push the cart,
Which keeps your hands
    Occupied
While your husband
Speed shops
With his list.

On this occasion
My sister
Was your spotter
—Following you
As you meandered
Through the aisles.
Shaking her head—
"No"
For each miscellaneous item
You held up for approval.

She told me
About your dance

Up the aisle
When you rounded the corner
And saw
    The love of your life!
How you swayed and sashayed
Wagging your finger
At him
And smiling.

Every Day is a Holiday

I ask my father
About his day.
He tells me
Every day
Is a holiday.

Dementia 101

Both day
And night
—You only sleep now.
Winding down,
Or so we've told ourselves.
Until I recall
The first rule of dementia—
When changes arise
Check for a UTI.

Painful

You wince
And complain
About a pain
In your side
—The same side
With the ribs you broke
Last fall—
The last time you fell.
You fractured two ribs
In three places
And never once
Complained.
But now?
Has the pain
Center
In your brain
Reengaged?
Or is this something
New?
It is impossible
To know
—And painful
To not know.

Love Without Borders

You didn't want me to mail
My dissolution of marriage
Announcement;
Such things weren't done.
I did it anyway.

You didn't want me to date
A man
Shorter than I am;
I didn't bother
To ask you why?

You didn't want me to love
A woman;
You gave me your blessing
Anyway.

You worried
For my happiness
        —The thing you wanted most
For me.
Anything else
You told me
Was your insecurity—
A fear
Of what your friends
Would say.

They'd say
They love you
        —And they love me, too.
A few were at your home
Last night;
They brought a party
With their cheer
—Crab and cake—
They did it
For love's sake.

A Biopsy of Fear

Your husband
Took you to the dermatologist
Because the appointment
    Was on his calendar.

He didn't think
—To cancel it.
He didn't think
It through.

A doctor examined
And biopsied you;
That's what they do.

But what will we do
When they tell us
You have cancer?
And forced to answer
We must decide
To act
    —Or let it ride.

Good Medicine

Your husband doles out
Your pills
This morning
And explains each one
As if the routine
Were new.

"This one
Is for your heart;
And this one is a vitamin."

He modulates his voice
Smooth and enticing;
You do not like
Taking pills
So he asks you
If a kiss with them would help.

Not falling for his tricks
But following his lead
You smile coyly
And reply—
*"I'd rather
Wrap up with you in bed."*

He kisses you
And laughs
Then asks—
"Would you like another
Little kiss?"

Drawing out your answer
"Sure!"
You pucker up and wait.

Thank you for Asking

My father
Gives you a choice—
Your friends
Have invited you to dinner.

He asks if you prefer
To go to their home?
Or have them come to you?

You do not express a preference
Only your approval
At having been considered—
*"You better be glad you asked me
Or I would have bopped you one."*

In this
You're right—
Everyone likes to be asked.

Slow Food

"Here it comes!
Open up."

My father feeds you
—Most meals an exercise
    In patience.
With humor
He shares his running commentary—
"It only took four tries
But we got it.
Not to worry."

He asks you again—
"Are you ready for a bite of egg?"
You tell him
Your stomach has been belly-whopped.
Without missing a beat
He tells you

Your smoothie is the remedy
For a stomach
That's been belly-whopped.

I concur
—You don't.

*"You lie,
She lies;
You all lie."*

He raises a new bite to your lips.
"It's very helpful when you open
Your eyes
    —And your mouth.
Can you multitask?"

You protest—
*"Mary!
Get that dead chicken
Off of me!"*

He assures you
It's not the chicken
It's the egg
And asks you again—
"Are you ready?"

*"Yeah
Sure."*

And so it goes—
You chew
And chew
And chew
—Eyes closed;

While he hovers a new forkful
In front of your lips
Waiting patiently to begin the process
—Again.

Poor Richard

I heard from my father
A full accounting of the mess you made.
How the night before last
You poured your Ensure
All over the table.
How when he said—
"Oh my, you spilled your drink!"
You corrected him—
*"No.
I poured it."*

I was there last night
When you poured your Ensure again.
Your husband returned from the sink—
"Well, I'll be damned,
You've got that down."

"Les, this isn't a good procedure.
It makes a big mess and it stains.
It doesn't make me happy."

He pauses.
"Oh well—
If it makes you happy."
He spoke out loud to you,
But he was speaking to himself—
"In the big scheme of things

It doesn't matter,
And we're working
With the total scheme."

"The ants will be doing a happy dance."

He sighs,
And recommends
That if you have a choice
You drink your drinks.

Signing off with me,
He leans into the iPad
And shakes his head—
"I'm glad she doesn't spill things anymore
    She just pours them out
—She's progressing."

Role Models

Your friend sent me a note
And shared how both of you
—Your husband and you—
"Are role models to all of us
On dealing with life
When the going gets tough."
It's true.
Just like your husband sings—

    "Anyone can smile
    When life goes along
    Like a song,
    But the man who's worthwhile
    Is the man who can smile

When everything in life
goes wrong."

Thank You

My father
Mailed me your notecards.
You never liked to write—
A post-it note that said
"Love, mom"
Sufficed for correspondence.

Preaching etiquette
You modeled procrastination.
And when duty demanded
.   A letter
You called me for my help.

Today I give it freely
Happy to write notes
Of gratitude
To all your friends
On your behalf
      —My own,
Your husband's
And our family's.

No Whining

Comparing notes
With my sister
I tell her you're back;
Your UTI is gone

Your will to live returned—
And with that will
Your many moods.
I prefer
The witty,
Feisty you
To the little girl
That whines.
My sister gives me
Her advice;
She tells you
So she tells me—
"Mom
You're whining;
I don't do whining."
Simple and straightforward
Apparently
You never disagree
        —I'll have to see
If this will work for me.

Your Eyes

They say the eyes
Are windows
To the soul;
        Yours
Remind me
Of a cat—
Busy tracking things
None of us can see.

My sister says she melts
When you look at her
With your "big bug eyes"
Exaggerated
    By your sunken face.
Magnified this evening
By glasses
Two sizes
Too large.

You like to wear
Your husband's spectacles
Whenever he sets them down.
He cannot see
Without them;
I wonder what you see
With them.
I ask you how they work
And you tell me—
They're just fine.

Wedding Bells

You married my father
Fifty-seven years ago
On the third of September.
It was a small affair
On a Tuesday night
With a hand-me-down ring.
You don't remember this,
So you tell him one evening
As you strolled up the lane
That you'd like to get married.

He told you okay—
And figured that was that.
  But it wasn't.
You brought it up again
The next day
And then again
The next.
You brought it up every day,
So yesterday
He made some plans.
The ceremony will be private
The way you say you want it.
A good friend will marry you
And another will be your witness.
Your husband bought you flowers
And prepared a luncheon for four.
He'll give you a shower
And style your hair—
Then today at eleven,
The two or you
Will renew
A love forever true.

Shifting Blame

There was a turd
In your diaper
But it wasn't
  —Yours.
You told your husband—
"I didn't do that."

He asked this morning
About finishing your egg;

85

You told him you tried to
But the egg told you—
"Go away
You bother me."

He'd never heard
Of a talking egg;
You shrugged—
"Well I'm sorry,
It did."

Your Short Term Memory Works Just Fine

Your husband put you to bed
And rubbed your feet
Like every night,
Only this night
You didn't fall asleep.

Reading in the other room
He heard you call out—
"Mother."
When he came to you
You told him—
"I love you."
He kissed you and left again.

Ten minutes passed
And you called
    Again—
This time for Rody.
You didn't want anything
So he kissed you

Then left once more.

He settled back into his book
—You called for him again;
    And then again.
Finally, he said to you—
"Now look,
This is the fifth time
You've called me in here."

Prone to exaggerate
You set him straight—
*"No,
It's only the fourth."*

The Jury is Still Out

The word is out
About your marriage
And a friend stopped by
To say congratulations.
Like any new bride
You beamed
And showed her your ring.
But then you voiced your doubt—
*"I'm not sure
If It's going to work."*

What the End of the Tether Looks Like

Readers
Do not read this
If it will disturb you—

This was not an easy day.

Your husband put you to bed
Last night at eight;
He helped you to the bathroom
At ten.
From ten to four
You talked
Pleaded
Pulled the covers
    —And probably cried.
You were up
Showered and dressed
By six.

The morning began with you
"Carpet bombing"
The bathroom
In shit.
Vickie had the day off.

You have another UTI.
The antibiotics aren't working.
You slept all day;
    Your husband did not.
He helped you clear
The phlegm in your throat
With his fingers.
Then prepared a dinner
    You didn't eat.
You ate only enough
Breakfast and lunch
"To keep a sparrow alive"
He tells me.

Your eyes
And lips
Remained closed through dinner.
You refused your antibiotic
　　—Insisted you'd taken it already.
Your husband prayed
For patience.
Then asked me how long
Can a person live
　　Without eating?
He told me he is worried.
Then told me—
"Maybe it's because
I didn't get any sleep last night,
But I don't have the right attitude
　　Today.
I am a bit frustrated.
It's a good thing the end of my tether
　　Is a loop."

Looping

You slept
Twelve hours
Without
Turning over.

Your husband
Left
This morning
To play golf.
I told him
Today
Would be

A new day;
And it is.
Vickie asked you
This morning
How it feels
To be married.
You smiled wide
And replied—
"Yeah,
But it ain't easy
For him."

Moonlight Fills His Hands

If you want to understand
Your husband's
Love—
Listen,
Really listen
To *The Man of La Mancha.*

You are his Dulcinea
—That he alone can name.

   "For with his Dulcinea
   Beside him so to stand,
   A man can do quite anything,
   Outfly the bird upon the wing,
   Hold moonlight in his hand.
   Yet if you build your life on dreams
   It's prudent to recall,
   A man with moonlight in his hand
   Has nothing there at all.
   There is no Dulcinea,

She's made of flame and air,
And yet how lovely life would seem
If ev'ry man could weave a dream
To keep him from despair.
To each his Dulcinea ...
Though she's naught but flame and air."

You wonder why he loves you
    His Dulcinea;
His catalyst to dream.
You keep him from despair—
For you
He can do anything
—And every day
    He does.

These Questions Are Not Easy

Last night
You would not take your pill—
Pursed your lips
Spit it out
Insisted you'd taken it already
—Your usual variety of
    No.
Your husband mused
Aloud—
"I wonder what would happen
If we let her live
With a UTI?"

Without really hearing
Him,
I automatically

Replied—
"Pneumonia and UTIs
Are the two leading causes of
        I paused
Awkwardly
Unable to say
Death
In front of you,
And so instead
I said—
"The end."

Your husband said—
"I know."
Then neither of us
Said anything
More.
The moment
Passed
—But not
Unnoticed.

Had I heard
What I thought
I heard?
Or did I imagine
What I needed
To hear?
On the iPad
It is so easy
To mishear.

Your bacteria grow
Resilient;
We fight a losing battle
In a war

We will not win.
The UTI is not
Uncomfortable
For you
—You sleep a great deal more
And eat
    Even less.

Does your husband
Keep you alive
For your sake
    Or for his own?
If he chooses
To let you go—
Does he choose
For you,
    Or for himself?
I know these are the questions
He grapples with.
Questions with answers
Only he can know.
I wish the world
—This were not so.

Not Yet

This is not the poem
I wrote today;
Not the verse
Tearing at my heart.

Blinded by tears
Raw
With emotion

And fear
I went to the edge
—And looked over.

I saw where you are going
And I know
I'll let you go.
But now
Is not that moment,
And I leave my verse
Unsaid—

"Don't cross your bridges
Before you get to them."
—Your standard refrain
Running through
My head.

Your Good Side

Your husband
Helped you rise
From the couch.
He gave you his arm
And made a show
Of gallantly
Escorting you
To the table.

You smiled
And asked—
"Are you trying
To get on my good side?"

He laughed—
"Well yes,
I am."

You told him—
*"It's not an
Unreachable
Goal."*

We Carry On

The cyclical sadness
Of the world
Is at a zenith these days
—I feel this
Just as I feel you
    Retreating.
I feel the frayed and fragile
Tether
That holds all of us
    Together
And wonder how much
Can I bear?
This daily vulnerability
We wear
Weighs heavily
On tired shoulders
—Bruising further
This bleeding heart.

Why I Wake Early

I read poetry
To you
And Dad
After dinner.
I read from
Mary Oliver
Why I Wake Early.
She reminds me
Of you,
The way you taught me
To notice
And love—
Your love
For nature.
I read you
The title poem;
A poem of gratitude
And blessing.
I read you *Bones,*
A poem of wondering
And wonder.
I read you *Bean,*
A lesson in virtue.
I finished with
Arrowhead,
The impeccable voice
Of our conscience.
These things you gave
To me—
I now give back
To you.

Your Angel

In the beginning,
When your mind
Still reasoned
And you knew
What lay in store
For you,
We talked about
Your guardian angel.
I told you
She was always with you;
That you didn't need
To be afraid.

She is
And you don't.
You were crying
Inconsolably
On your bed
Sobbing and calling
For mother.

Vickie knew
Exactly what to do.
From her cell phone
She called your house phone
And handed it to you.

You stopped crying
And said—
"Hello?"

Standing just outside
Your room

Vickie answered you—
"Hello Lesley,
This is your friend.
Are you having a nice day?"

"Yeah. But I'm afraid."

"Don't you have somebody
There with you?"

"Yes, Vickie's here."

"Well then,
You and Vickie
Go have a good day."

"Okay, I guess I can do that;
But I don't have any way
To go anywhere."

"Don't you have a red car
 In the driveway?"

You went to the window
And looked out.
"Yeah."

"Well get in the car ,
Go for a ride
And have a good day."

You said goodbye
And hung up.
A little while later
You went out
And got in the car.

Together,
You and your angel
—Had a good day.

Will You Be My Mother

You were calling
For your mother
And Vickie gently
Reminded you
—She's gone.

You sniffled—
"Nobody
Takes me seriously.

Will you be my mother?"

You gave her a hug
And told her—
"I really do appreciate
Everything you do.
I really do."

Oh—

Helping my father dress you
This morning—
You were working up
    To a good cry.
You began with a
Distressed and pitiful—
"Oh"

—"Oh! Sweet mystery
Of life
At last you've found me."

Your husband
Began singing
—A joyful baritone—
And leaned in for a kiss.

"That's the song
You were going to sing
Right?"

Mistaken Identity

In a convenient case
Of mistaken identity
You fussed at me
Using my sister's name
—My reputation
Left innocent
And free of blame.

How You See Me

Now that you're a bride
You're pregnant, too!
The baby is due
In October
According to you.
Vickie asked
If you prefer a boy
Or a girl?

Mixing the past
And present
You tell us,
You had one of each.
"That's right"
I chime in—
"You had a boy
And a girl
—Then you had me."
Joking with you
I claimed
That I am a category
All of my own.
In a familiar voice,
Straight out of our past
You whole-heartedly
Agreed—

"Lord, yes!"

Rest in Peace

When I kiss you
Goodnight
I no longer tell you
That I will see you
In the morning.
Instead,
I whisper
In your ear
That I hope you dream
Of angels
And return
To the stars.

My father and I
Rub your feet
And as you begin to snore
Each of us
Silently
Reassures you
That it's okay
　　To leave.
You have lived well;
Are loved well
And will forever
　　Be alive
In our hearts.
You do not
Need to stay
—We will, all of us,
Be okay.

Witness

I attended the birth
Of a dear friend's
Third child—
The hardest work
I've ever done.
Witness
To life's fiercest truth.
A challenging pregnancy,
With a difficult labor.
I held a space
And modeled calm
Through endless hours
Of constant struggle
In the face
Of a fathomless fear.

And in the end,
A healthy boy
Was born—
A new life begun.
I think of that beginning
When I think of your ending.
Witness to life's fiercest truth;
Doula to your death.
This is the real work
We spend our lives
Preparing for—
    Witnesses
To life's fiercest truth.

DNR

Department of
Natural Resources
    Our own.
Do Not Resuscitate
Begins at home.
It means
Do Not Ring
911.
We pray that you'll die
While you sleep,
And prepare ourselves
In the event
    That you don't.
We do not wish
For you to die
A medical death
Rushed in an ambulance
Surrounded by strangers

Tasked with doing
What we could not.
And so we talk of courage
And pray for ourselves
That if the moment
When death comes for you
Comes with violence
We will not violate
Your sacred trust
In us
To hold your hand
And let you die
With dignity
At home
—And not alone.

The Poet and the Pragmatist

Your husband
Walks into the room
   And seeing you
He smiles and delivers
His favorite line—
"Lesley!
Have you been taking
Pretty pills again?
You look lovely!"
True to form
You fix him with a look
That says
Get real!

And reply—
*"Richard
You lie like a rock."*

Refusing Love

I went to the Amish market
Then the produce stand
Gathering ingredients
You once enjoyed.
I tell you my plans
To make spareribs,
Succotash
And a fresh peach pie.

You tell me—
*"You can put
Whatever you like
In front of me
But it doesn't mean
I'll open my mouth."*

How well I know this.
At 84 pounds
And vanishing
    Daily
I cook
Not to sustain
Your life
But to nourish
Our souls.

The Mystery of Your Mind

When we left the house
For our morning walk
You commented
That the air felt like rain—
I could have said the same.

We ran into your neighbor
Who told us of her plans
To spend the weekend
Emptying her parents' home.
Surprising us both,
You responded with empathy
    And clarity—
"That's not fun;
That's difficult work."

And then
—Not a moment later,
As we continued on our way,
You waved and called out—
"Good morning"
To the yellow fire hydrant.

The Rebel in You

You resent
Being told what to do.
From the moment
You rise
    It begins.
We dress you
Then coax you

Toward the kitchen
And breakfast.
You take your time
    Distracted
And resistant.

You tell me—
"Oh,
Here we go again—
Do this Lesley;
Don't do that."

At the table
    Three meals a day
You seal your lips
Say no
And push our hands
Away.
We persist—
You don't always mean
What you say.
So after dinner
My father stepped away
And left you seated still
With your glass of Ensure
More than half full.
When he returned
To his surprise
The glass was empty
—A victory!

He carried on and on.
Told you how proud he was
—What a good thing
You had done!
    The rebel in you

Smiled sweetly
Accepting all his accolades.
Your emptied glass
    Emptied
Into the pocket of your apron
—Had yet to be discovered.

What a Wonderful Life

We were not talking
    About sex
So we laughed, when out of the blue
You told us—
*"No screwing in the kitchen,
That's not nice!"*

My father smiled at you
    Mischievous
With a twinkle in his eye—
"Have you ever screwed in the kitchen Lesley?"

You returned his sly smile
With one of your own
Your answer
Rolling out playfully slow—
"Sure."

My father winked at me—
"That's how you got to be
The tall girl in the kitchen
    —It was meant to be."

He looked back at you—

"What a wonderful life.
We made a lot of great love
Didn't we? We still do."

You beamed back him—
*"Yeah,
We're good love makers."*

Your Example

You took issue
With my independent spirit
    —A quality I learned from you
Who married
Fifty-seven years ago
Today
The man you chose
—Despite your father saying
    No.

He told your husband
He wasn't good enough
And pointed out his flaws.
A terrible student
With a dubious reputation
And no money to his name,
He assumed he'd bring you only
Heartbreak and shame.

Strong-willed
And sure of yourself
You chose instead
To live your own way

That day
And every day.
To follow your heart—
    Until death do you part.

Upon Reflection

Growing up
You made me
Self-conscious
Of my looks.
I never passed
A mirror
    Without looking.
I felt your scrutiny
And my inadequacy—
But never stopped
To wonder
—How it was
You saw yourself?

I watch you now—
You never pass a mirror
    Without looking.
And I wonder
How do you see
Yourself?

I asked you today
While you gazed
At your reflection
Who you saw
—And how you felt.
You didn't answer me;

You said instead—
"Come on, let's go."

Then when I turned
To walk away
I heard you say—
"You have a fat hiney."

I spun around—
"What did you say?"

"You have a fat hiney."

And I see at last
That who I saw
Was only your reflection
—The way you felt
About
    Yourself.

Why You Stay

On our walk the other day
You told me—
*"I can't wait
To get my old life back."*

Taken aback—
I wonder what keeps you here?
When I look at you
And see only skin and bones
—I wonder why
You stay?

Then I see all the friends
That come by—
The way they adore you;
The memories you share
    The love that's still there.
And I remember—

Why are any of us here?
The answer
    —Is Love.

Jekyll & Hyde

You were particularly
Unpleasant today
For one trying half hour.
Pushing
And hitting;
You called me
Stupid
Mean and ugly.
Told all of us
To get away.
You snarled
Taunted and mimicked
—Not even the dog
Avoided the fray.

Full Moon and Madness

*"I'm sorry—
But I hope I keep you up
Half the night!"*

It will probably
Be all night.
Perhaps it's the moon
—Or just one of those nights.

According to you—
    Everyone is lying
And nothing I say
Stops you from crying.

A Final Feast

We had a crab feast
Yesterday
To celebrate summer

    And you—
Sat down at the table
In front of a pile of crabs
And knew
Exactly what to do.

You pounded away
And sucked crab meat
From claws.
Ate every bite
Of lump back fin
With a huge grin
And messy hands.

We relished
Your joy
And stored away
A memory of this day

—Your final feast
The Eastern Shore way.
Corn, crabs and Old Bay—
The seasoning
Of our love
For this time and place
—We've shared
With you.

Breathing in Love

I drove away today
Not knowing
If I'd hold you ever again;
    Your skeleton
Covered in skin
Like the dried leaves
You gathered on our walk—
    Brittle with decay.
You decompose before our eyes
Until one day
—Like dust
Your breath
Will mingle with our own.

Goodbye

I packed my car
Then sat with you
On the couch
For an hour.
I rubbed your head;
We napped.

When it was time to leave
I rubbed your chest
And told you—
"I am always in your heart
And you're in mine."

You replied—
"That's nice.
You're going to have a grand time
—But don't come home with a husband.

Now get your keys and get out of here."

When I'm Not There

Your husband ran into a friend
Shopping at Walmart.
His wife also suffers
With Parkinson's
And they commiserated.

Unlike your husband,
He told yours—
    He likes to cook.
He asked him if he had a rice cooker
Then confidently said—
"Follow me."

He picked one out
And handed it to your husband—
"You'll be a gourmet cook
With the push of one button."

I asked your husband—
"Do you even like rice?"
He answered—
 "I do now."

He tells me all this
While we configure
His new Wi-Fi—
I am the tall girl in the kitchen
—Plus tech support.

When we finally finish
 Dinner is ruined.
Burned sauce
Burned rice
—And you are crying.

He offers you a banana.

Then turns to the iPad and asks—
"When are you coming back?"

Your Swan Song

There is a swan
That glides
Up Cemetery Cove
—The morbid address
For your mortal end.

You scolded Vickie
First thing yesterday
For not wearing
—Her dancing shoes.

When you finally
Made it to the kitchen
Dressed
And ready for a new day
Your husband
Announced your arrival.

You held on to Vickie
And did the cancan
Kicking your right leg high
    Over and over.

Then to our laughter
And applause
    You struck a pose—
One hand on your hip
The other
Seductively
Behind your head.

Your swan song—
The way I will remember
You
Playful and sexy
    Delighting
In delighting us.

Pregnant with My Love for You

Out of the blue
I was pregnant
    —Then it was you.
You told everyone
After the wedding

That you were due
A baby in October.

But then you changed
Your mind;
Told me,
You didn't want to be.
So I told you
You weren't,
And now
—It's back to me.

Over dinner
You told my father
    I'm pregnant—
Told him to ask me.
He did,
And I didn't
Know what to say.

Instead I asked—
"Do you want me to be?"

As if I'd asked the obvious
You fired back—
"Of course I do!
—You big sissy!"

I don't understand,
But I do
    Agree
Motherhood
—I've learned
From loving you—
Takes strength
And courage too.

You Can Be a Real Pill

Your husband gave you your pill
—You spit it out
And grinned.
He asked you—
"What's the grin about?"
You told him—
"I got one up on you."

He asked you—
"Are you ready
For this pill?
It's an important one,
It keeps you
From coughing."

You said—
"Okay,"
Then added—
"But anyone else
Who would like it
Can have it."

I'm on the iPad
Listening
To him
Plead with you
     Again
To take your pills.
As tired of hearing
The same lines
As we grow
From saying them,
You snap—

"Then Page says
This is the
La-s-s-s-s-t one;
Well, Phhhh!"

And then again
This morning,
Variations
On a theme
He asks you—
"Lesley, have you taken
Your pills yet?"
You tell him—
"No.
But I've thought a lot
About it."

He suggests
You take them,
And I weigh in
Concurring.
　　You don't—
"Will both of you
Go to—"
You pause
Searching for the word—
"South America."

My father
Looks at me
—I look at him,
And we agree—
South America
Sounds great!

Stairway to Heaven

Thankfully,
You have not been
    A wanderer.
The stairs—
However
—These are your favorite
Hazard.
It only takes
A moment
Of not watching
You
To find
You're halfway
Up the stairs—
Both hands gripping
The banister;
Your feet crossed
As your mind
    Untangles
Your next step.

Perfect in Every Way

I am certain
Some days
That you
Understand
More than
I know.

—I know
You listen to
Every word
We say.
But I can't
Imagine
What you
Are thinking,
Or feeling—
We speak
As if
You aren't there.

Your deadpan
Wit—
    When it shows up
—Silences
Us.
Astonished
And humbled,
You are
    Less than
You were—
    And more than
You appear to be.
So we love you
As though
    You are perfect.
—Your husband's
Favorite thing
To say—
"You're perfect
In every way."

A Funeral with Your Name On It

You were listening
To me
Tell your husband
About a service—
    The word I used
And you mumbled
To no one
In particular—
"There's a funeral
With my name on it."

When the Color has Left Your Cheeks

Your friend
Made me a quilt;
Asked me
What my colors are.
    Boring
According to you.
Black,
White
And shades of grey.

There will be grey days
When you're gone
And it will be
    My comfort quilt.
A choreograph
Of patterns and shapes—
Patches
Of memory
Sewn into

A loving embrace;
The feeling
Of you.

Peace Out

I am left
Virtually
Alone
With you—
The iPad
On its stand;
You sitting
Across from me
At the kitchen table.

You pick me up—
Begin to
Rearrange
Me.
Nothing
Safe
From your need
To rearrange.

This has happened
Before.
I call out to you
Urgently
As your unsteady
Hands
Carry me
Nowhere
In particular.

"Mom!
Mom!!
Put me down;
Put me back!"
It takes a while
—You say nothing
And I can't know
If you hear me.

Eventually
The view
Steadies,
And the iPad
Is back in its stand.

I exhale
The breath
I was holding,
But still
You have said
Nothing.
From off screen,
Your hand appears
—You flash me
    The peace sign
And wander off.

Why Now?

Where does this
Wit
Of yours
Come from?

Why did you
Never
Share it before?
Why didn't you
Make us laugh
The way you do
Now?

I wonder
Who you wanted to be?
I wonder
Who you could have been?
I wonder
Who I might have been?

You were everyone
To me;
I see the world
Through you—
Exactly
As you taught me to.

The Truth

I asked you—
"How was your walk?"

You answered—
"So slow
You could hardly tell
Anyone was moving."

One of These Mornings You'll Be Gone

Your husband called me
    In my dream
This afternoon
—He told me
You had passed.
Passed—
The word
He used;
And I realize
I don't know
What word
He will use.
I woke
With a start
—Then waited
All afternoon
For his call.
It came at dinnertime
The same
As every night.
I wait
—And don't

With
Every breath
And know—
    That no,
I can't imagine
How my life
Will feel;
How I will feel
When you're not
Here.

Fun and Games

Your husband
Was calling your name—
You walked by him
    And said nothing.
When you entered
The next room
You told Vickie
You were hiding
From him.
Giddy and giggling—
"I'm going to hide;
I'm going to hide."

Carefully
Slowly
You lowered yourself
On to all fours
In front of a wingback chair
Then buried your face
In the cushions—
    Hidden.

Your husband
Played along,
Came into the room
Calling—
"Lesley,
Where are you?"
When he found you,
You laughed
And laughed.
    Everyone laughed.
Yesterday
—Was a good day.

Breathing Lessons

My father was late
Calling
This morning.
I lingered
In bed
    Breathing—
Imagining
How I will feel.

When he does call
His face
Is somber.
I am accustomed
To this—
Like a weather man
On location
Waiting
For the camera
To go live,

He stares into the iPad
And waits
For our video
    To connect.

His expression
is serious
As he tells me
    The weather
Every morning—
There,
Here
And in Alaska.
Finally he smiles,
Tells me
Good morning;
And our conversation
Begins.

I realize
That his face
When he calls
To tell me
You are gone
Will resemble
His meteorologist look.

I cannot
Know
In advance
What will come
When he opens
His mouth
To speak.

Each morning
I see his face,
My heart slows—
    And I wait.
I am
Constantly
Conditioning
For your
Death—
Remembering
    To breathe.
Like an expectant
Mother
Practicing
For a pain
She cannot
Imagine
—But knows
Is coming.

Rebirth

There was a discussion
This morning
About my birthday
Tomorrow.
You asked Vickie
To repeat my age
—I will be 46.
You stated
Incredulous—
"That old?"

There are so many ways
I could interpret
That—
Too many.

Instead,
I smile
Knowing
None of them
Are true;
All of them
Could be;
And I'll never know—
So I let it go
—And go on
Smiling.

Happy! Happy! Happiest!

No somber meteorologist
This morning.
I waited in bed
For your call.
Your husband
Ushered you
To your seat at the table
Then put his foot
On his gutbucket
And the two of you
Began;
Sang Happy Birthday—
Not once,
But three times.
You sang

All the words.
And I have no
Words
For how happy
I feel
To be alive
   And in love
With loving
You.

Death's Door

I revised
My life
Plan
Today;
Thought about
   After
You're gone.
How death
Only announces
   The beginning.
So much
History
To catalog
And give
   New life.
So much
About you
To discover.
To uncover
Who you
Were,
Weren't

And
Are
    —To me.
In your death
This opening door—
And a path
I never saw
Before.

Dynamite

Your husband told me
This morning
You have a new code;
You told him—
"I think I need dynamite."

He guessed correctly
What that meant
And led you
To the bathroom.

The morning before
Was memorable—
    Explosive!
He called it your
—Poo de grâce.

We talk a lot
About your bowels
And confess
How secretly we hope
Each day
You'll go

On someone else's watch.
We joke
About winning
Your lottery
—And make light
Of life's
Unpleasantness.

Resistance Training

I've spent my life
Developing
    Core strength
Through my resistance
To your opposition.

Timing
And strategizing
The delivery
Of my ideas.

Always practical,
Your critical eye
Saw faults
And flaws
—While in my enthusiasm
I see everywhere
    Only
Blue skies.

But last night
I jumped in
Without preamble
    Or caution

And shared
My new life plan.
You heard every word—
You said nothing.
It felt strange
—You being there,
    But not there.
No struggle
Between us;
No need
To justify my right
    To be
—Excited.

No longer
In training.

No longer
Your child.

A Subconscious View

I dropped a pill
I was lifting
To your lips
And said—
"Whoops."

You responded—
"I'm sorry Page
That you did that,
But I'm thrilled
—Because you're perfect."

For the first time
I consider
That I made you
—Self-conscious,
Too.

When No One Listens to You

"How come
You all are telling me
What to do
Again?"

I try to imagine
What that's like
For you
　　　—I can't.
You were
In charge
Once—
Of us,
This house
And of yourself.

"Here I go
Being bossed
again—
Well, I'm not
Going to have it."

You put your foot
Down
　　Daily

—We laugh
And nothing changes.

"Get out of my mouth!
Or I'll slap you all down.
I am so sick
Of you putting
Your hands
In my face.
If you don't like it
Tough titty!"

We don't;
You don't
—We don't have
A choice.

"You can only
Think of one thing
—Day after day
Like a little dope addict.
Take your pills,
Eat your dinner—
Wah, wah, wah, wah."

We don't listen
To you
        —We can't.
And I can't
Imagine
What that's like
For you.

Wise Innocence

Your grandchildren
Are coming to visit
From Alaska
And your husband
Is putting them
    To work.

You tell him
That's not nice.

With a Cheshire grin
    He agrees.

Then he tells you—
"It was their idea."

You raise your fingers
To your forehead,
Wiggle them
And answer—
"Bull!"

Home Again

I get to see you
    Again.

You look healthy;
Are happy
    —Today.
Every day
Is a different

Day
And I am
Grateful
For each
And every one.

Showering with You

You designed your home
With a walk-in shower
    —For two.
No doubt
You never imagined
That the bare body
Next to you
    Would be mine.
I wash your hair
And gently lather
Your frail frame.
If your former self
Knew,
She would be
    Mortified—
Consider it
Undignified.
Perhaps
My former self
Would have felt
The same;
    Known shame.
But not today.
Now I see
Only
The nobility

In knowing
The naked
Reality
    Of Love
In every form.

In Bed with You

I lingered in bed—
    Yours.
I came downstairs
This morning
When the clock struck
Eight
And plopped down
In the sliver of space
Between your husband
    And you.
We snuggled
And giggled;
I told you my dreams—
You told me yours.

Consequences

There are consequences
To caregiving.
I accompanied
My father
To the doctor today.
Four years
Of bending,
Twisting

And lifting you
    Up
Out of bed;
Lowering you
    Down
To sit,
Then raising you
    Again—
There are consequences
To caregiving.
The doctor ordered
    Rest
—An impossible
Request.

Screwed Up

You wouldn't
Get out of bed
This morning.
We all took turns
Trying
To coax you
And convince you.
I lay down
With the cat
The dog
And you.

You asked me—
*"How would you like
To be told
When to screw?"*

Your hallucinations—
So you tell us
—Tell you
What to do.
They want you
To *"screw"*
Outdoors
—With everybody
Watching.

You tell me—
"Sex should be
Spontaneous;
Unscripted
Is much better."

I try to reassure you—
To dispel your delusions.
I tell you
Not to worry
    That no one
Is having sex.
To which you reply—
"Well then, I'm leaving."

Two Views

We woke you
Early
This morning.
Packed a picnic
And headed out
In search
Of a view

For the lunar eclipse.
We chose a spot
At the end of town
Overlooking
The water
And watched
The light
Of the moon
    Slowly
—Recede
Into shadow.
Coming home
We parked
In the field
And watched
The sun
    Slowly
—Rise.

Breaking with Western Medicine

You tripped
Yesterday.
My back
To you—
I heard your head
    Hit the floor.

This is not
The first time,
Though it's been
A long time.

You were sore,

Like before;
Nothing more.
Bones
Against bare floor
        —Our worst fear
But still
You are here.
We wonder
How can it be?
The answer
We think
Is your drink—

Chia seeds
Flax seeds
Goji berries
Cinnamon
Barley grass
Kale, collards or chard
Parsley
Almonds
Dates
Blueberries
Cranberries
Honey
Seaweed
Banana
Apple
Coconut water

And love!—

Your husband's
Daily elixir
Blended

To keep you
    Pill free
And alive.

Letting Go of Letting Go

The art
Of letting go
Includes
Letting go
—Of letting go.

Each time
We make peace
With losing you
You seem
To make peace
With staying.

This new serenity
In you
—A mirror
Of our own.
Set free
In our hearts
And minds,
Your vitality
Returns
Us to this present.
Reminds
Us to be present
With you
—Here
Now—

As you are
For as long as
You will be.

Your Environmental Impact

Diapers
Disposable gloves
Feminine wipes
And plastic bags.
Clorox wipes
And paper towels.
Soiled clothes, bedding and towels
    —The extra loads of laundry.
Wasted, uneaten
Food.
Daily car rides
    To nowhere.
The running water
You turn on
    Then don't turn off.
The things you bought
    And didn't need—
Before we knew.
The things we need
    You threw away
Without us knowing.

Significant

You confuse
    A significant
Portion

Of the words
You use,
Yet when I asked
Your husband
How to spell
    Significant
It was you
Who,
Eyes closed,
Replied—
    S.i.g.n.i.f.i.c.a.n.t.
An accomplishment
I find
Far
—From insignificant.

Reminiscing

We took you
To Ocean City today.
A sunny, warm
October day.
We walked along
The boardwalk,
Glad to be there
Without
The crowds.

I'd never been—
You hadn't been
    In years.
Your husband and you
Spent summers
Visiting

As kids.
He told us
Stories
Of the jobs he had
Mixing sodas
And putting out
Umbrellas.
Of renting a room
In a boarding house
    Attic
For a dollar
A night
—When everything
Was beach
And the boardwalk
Ended
At twelfth street.

I put my feet
In the ocean
    —For you;
Felt healed
And renewed
    Together—
With you.

Are We Evolving?

I return
To the question
Of are you
    Devolving?
Or could you be
    Evolving?

How do we know?

You show us
Daily
    How little
    We know;
Teach us
Daily
To stop
    Thinking
    We know
—Anything
About
What will be.

They say
The elderly
Lose their sense
Of smell—
You never
Had one;
    Now you do.

On the boardwalk
Yesterday
You announced—
"I like doughnuts."

A random comment
—So we believed.
Then farther down
The boardwalk
    I saw
What you could
Smell.

Yet even my eyes
Fail to see
All that you
Perceive—
People and scenes
Undetectable
To us.

You hear
Better than
We do;
So well,
We joke
You hear
Our thoughts.

I know no answers
To explain
The anomaly
You have become,
So I hold you
In my mind
    With humility
And wonder—
    Will we evolve
—With you?

Worried Sick

I wonder
If a lifetime
Of constant
    Worry
Brought on

Your current
Condition.

This conditioned
Response
    We all share—
Worrying
About
Everything
And anything.

Darkness fell
And you told me—
"This is the time
Of night
When I get scared."

I asked you why?
And you replied—
"I worry about
The children
Getting home."

I assured you
That the children
Were fine,
You had nothing
To fear.

Then you told me—
"I know;
I know I don't need
To worry,
But I've got a good case
Of the worries."

You told me then—
"I'm working on it,
But it takes time."

And I wonder—
When we heal
    Our worries
Do we heal
Our minds?

Mothers and Daughters

I learned
To love you
    Unconditionally.
I came
To understand
You.

I learned how
To be
With you—
To be
There for you.

I gained
All this
And more
By caring
    For someone else's
Mother
—Loving her
As if she were
My own.

I learned
How it feels
   To grow old;
What it means
To regret.

I learned how
   To forget
The past
And treasure
Right now.

I learned how
To enjoy
— You.

Love knows
No boundaries
And our teachers
Come
Unbidden,
In unexpected
Ways
When we need them
Most.

My teacher
Came into my life
Two years ago
— And left
This morning;
Her work
   Complete.
Because of what
She gave me

—My love for you
Feels complete too.

Why Not?

You told me
This morning—
"I am doing much better."

You are.

You asked
For a second
Piece of toast
With jam
And ate
Every bite.

You are eating
Larger portions—
    At every meal.
Laughing,
Smiling
And alert.

You recounted
Over breakfast
What a good time
We shared
Yesterday.
Remembered
Who was here,
And told me—
"It was wonderful!"

It was—
　And so are you.

I wonder
—Are there limits
To what love
Can do?

Granny Rocks!

You chose
With your first
Granddaughter
To be called
　Granny
—A tongue-in-cheek
Choice
Because you
Were anything
　But old—
Not yet
The woman
You've become.

On Sunday,
Each of us
Chose
A "Granny rock"
From your collection
　—A piece of you
To carry with us;
To carry for you.

The weight of
The world
You've known.
Places
And feelings
   Memories
Accumulated
—And enduring.

A lifetime
Of gathering,
Handed off—
   To be held
Safe
In the palm
Of our hands.
A marker
Of our love
For you.

We chose a tiny, red, heart-shaped rock for your
husband to carry in his pocket. He told you it was
perfect—because you stole his heart.

The Secret to a Good Time

Your husband
Always told us—
"A man is as happy
As he makes up
His mind to be."

We are
A happy three,

Your husband, you
And me—

Chatting
In gibberish
And non-sequiturs
About nothing.

Last night
You asked
If I had seen
The "hork fork."

After a reasonable
Effort
To find
Your reason
I turned
Instead
To having fun—
And so began
A round
Of puns.

I suggested that
The ork
Had made off
With your hork fork
To eat
His pork.

Your husband
Declared—
"The ork
Is a dork."

And so it goes—
Night after night,
A little reason,
The occasional rhyme—
And always
   A good time.

Slave to Love

Your husband and I
Looked at old photos
Of you.
We framed
His favorite.

When he saw it,
He proclaimed—
"Man!
Was she ever
A knockout.
I am such a lucky guy.
I am a slave to love.
   How else
—Could I do
What I do?"

When he showed
You
The photo
He said—
"That's my
Les-eee Baby!
Man!
Would I like to take her to bed."

You frowned
And replied—
"She's not tired."

Practicing Patience

Feeding you
Is a practice
In patience.
When you say—
"Yes"
You'd like a bite
To eat
You might mean
    No.
When you say—
"NO!"
You're just as likely
To open your lips
For another mouthful.

You chew
A thousand times;
    Pause—
And chew
Some more.

Three forkfuls in,
Then on the fourth
    You snarl—
*"I told you
When I walked in the door
That I don't like it."*

"You did?"
I suggest
That sometimes
We still eat
What we don't love.

Indignant!
You tell me—
"I beg your pardon
But I don't eat
What I don't like
And I'm sure you don't—
Hokey pokey."

I hand the fork
To your husband,
And you
   Open your mouth
For him.
Two more bites
—Then when your hands
Push his away,
He passes the fork
To me.

Another bite;
You glare
And declare—
"I'm going to rat on you
I'm telling you right now."

I ask who to?
And you reply—
"I don't know
But I'll figure it out."

I say okay,
Raise the fork
To your lips—
  You open wide.

Dreams and Conversations

I dreamt
Of you.
We were riding
A fire truck
Toward
Hel's Half Acre
—Toward
Your home
On Cemetery Cove.

You and I rode
On top
With six firemen
Wearing nothing
But towels
And smoking cigars.
The truck
Backed up to the creek
And tumbled us in.

I held you
In my arms—
Lifted
Your face
To the surface;

Then helped you
Climb out.

Together,
We knocked
On the door
At your lake house
    My new house
And entered.

There was a baby;
    Light streamed
    From its head.

You asked me—
"Did you see that
Baby?"

And then I woke.

Last night,
Our first conversation
    Since my dream
You asked
Your husband
And me—
"What happened
To the baby?
—We were going
To get a baby
For me."

Your husband repeats—
"A baby?"

"Yes"
You reply—
"A baby, baby
—From the aquarium."

Your husband repeats—
"The aquarium?"
You nod
Yes
And reply—
"Mee-ow."

The Sun Also Rises

I was still in bed
    Your bed
At the lake
When your husband
Called.
He asked
If I'd seen
The sunrise?
    I had.
From bed
I'd watched
Streaks of pink
And orange
Illuminate
The horizon—
Soaking it in
    My new view;
A reason to wake
Early.

You also rose
Early
    Last night.
We didn't know
You could do that,
Still—
    Lift yourself
Out of bed.

Your husband heard
A noise
An hour after
He'd seen you
To sleep.
He called out
And you
Answered.
You were occupied
Rearranging
In the dining room.

Your shoes and socks
On your bed,
Where your body
    Should have been;
Where you abandoned
Your notion
To put them on.

"Amazing things
Are going on
Down here"—
Your husband
Tells me.

I visualize
This morning's
Sunrise,
And concur—
There's magic going on
Here too.

The Practice of Being Happy

The cover
Of a yoga magazine
That someone left behind
Tells its audience
    To practice something.
I practice
    Being happy.
I practice
The yoga
    Of Love.
Same tenets—
Discipline
Focus
Balance
—Life
Itself
An exercise
In instability.

Halloween

You're going to a dinner party
For Halloween—
Your husband

Is selling snake oil;
You,
He's decided,
    Will be nine months pregnant.

This morning
Over breakfast
You tell Vickie—
*"I'm just doing
What I'm told."*

Your husband
Laughs—
"That's a first."

He tells you—
"If you like it,
It was my idea;
If you don't,
It was Page's."

Then he asks you—
"Whose idea was it?"

"Page's."

Your dead pan delivery
Is not
A dead giveaway
    Of anything—
And I wonder
How the old you
Would feel
About your costume
If she were
The new you?

Would she
Be willing
To break her mold
—And have fun too?

In Character

You brought
The house down
When you arrived
At the party
Pregnant.
Then you stole the show
When asked
At the table
If you wanted
A roll;
You wanted
To know—
"With who?"

Work. Work. Work.

All work
And no play
Makes granny dull
Again today.

When your husband
Shared
His plans to play golf,
You asked him—
"Are you kidding!?"

In your mind
There is endless
    Work
To accomplish
And none of us
Pitch in
Our share.
Your world
Has never
Been fair.

This is not
New
This obsession
With too much
To do;
Your addiction
To stress
And strain.
Too much to do
And too little time
—Your constant refrain.
What a shame.

Your Kingdom is a Royal Mess

My father brings the iPad
In close
And personal
To tell me
He has a serious
Problem
On his hands.

When you woke
From your two hour nap
He escorted you
To the bathroom
—You said
You needed
To go—
But then refused
To allow him
To lower your pants.

You told him—
*"You're not going to see
My kingdom."*

It's been two hours
He tells me,
And still
You won't go
—Not with him.

We laugh,
But know the truth—
　　It isn't funny.
Dirty diapers
Mean UTIs
And with your mind
In disarray
—Your kingdom
Is a mess.

Aware versus Able

Every evening
I ask you—
"How was your day?"
I don't expect you
To answer—
    You never do.

Last night,
However,
I phrased my question
A different way;
I wanted to know
What you and Vickie
Did that day.
I asked
Something
I never do,
I queried you—
    "Do you remember?"

Time passed;
I let it go.
You seemed troubled.
So your husband asked—
"What's the matter darling?"

You answered—
"Nothing.
I'm just trying to think
And it's giving me
A hard time."

Who can't relate to that?

I contemplate the difference
—the interconnection between
Your conscious
	Awareness;
Your cognitive
	Capacity;
Your verbal
	Capability.

Does your illness
Affect all three?

I know
—I can't
Always find
The word I want
	When I want it
Though I know
The meaning
I'm searching for.

Is it that way?
Do you know—
But can't say?

Room Service

Your husband
Went shopping
For warm bedding;
Bought you
A new down comforter
And flannel sheets.
He was telling me

All this
When you told him—
*"I have someone
Who tucks me in at night
And rubs my feet."*

Your husband smiled—
"They rub your feet?"

You smiled back
And answered with
A happy, drawn out—
"Yeah."

Sneaking Around

"Have you had any
Hugs and kisses
This morning?"
Your husband leans in
And you pucker up.

You tell him—
*"We can come out
Of the closet now."*

He raises an eyebrow—
"We're closet lovers?"

You smile
And ask him
Where he slept
Last night.

He tells you,
Then asks in return—
"Where did you sleep?
Maybe I can sneak in tonight."

You frown—
"I have to think about it."

Charades

You puff your cheeks
Like a blowfish
To indicate
You're full.
Blow on
—As if to blow
Away—
The glass,
The fork,
—Whatever we raise
To your lips—
To let us know
You mean
No.

Though you're able
To say—
"I'm cold,"
You clutch your arms,
Rattle your teeth,
Shiver and shake
In request of
More warmth.

You pull funny faces
In place of responses.
No translation
Required;
You express yourself
Best
When you don't say
A word.

Your Age is a Figure of Speech

Lost
In your imagined
World,
You tell us—
*"I can't believe
I let them talk me into—"*

Neither of us know
Who
Or
What
You speak of,
And like a radio
With poor reception,
Your meaning
Lapses.

When it comes through again
You say—
*"I'd like to think
I'm old enough
To know better."*

I wonder how old
You think
You are,
While your husband
Assures you
That age
Has nothing to do
    —With anything.

"I'm eleven months older,"
He shares—
"And just the other day
In Walmart
I let a friend
Talk me into buying
A rice cooker."

No One's Fool

Vickie
Has picked up
Your habit
Of winking
With a tongue click.
Your husband
Too.
They asked you
To show me
This morning.
You sat
Staring
—Motionless.

They continued
To click
And wink
And say—
"You do it Lesley,
Show Page.
Show Page
How you do it."

No wink.
No click.
A stony, silent
Stare—
As if you
Weren't
There;
Or don't care.

But they didn't
Stop—
So you
Raised your hands
Slowly,
Thoughtfully
And began
    To flap
Like a bird
Flying away.

This—

As the brain
Deteriorates,
A person's
Vocal projection
Diminishes.
The voice
Disappears.
This—
    Is to be expected.
This—
    Is what we were told.
Believed
And
Anticipated.
This—
    Is what happened;
No one
Could hear you.

But they didn't
Tell us
This—
    Nothing is a given;
Anything
Can change;
Rearrange.

Today,
Two years later,
You voice
A new view—
And everyone
Hears you.

Fifty Shades of Happy

Brimming with joy
My father
Breaks into song;
Begins to carry on.
I count how long
It takes
For you to say—
"Hush Richard!
You're putting on a show.
Why can't you be quiet?"

Your happy
　　Even now
Has limits;
Is calm and modest.
His knows
　　No bounds.
When he tells you—
"I'm so full of love
I need
To make a joyful noise,"
You tell him—
"Hush Richard,
You're so full
Of bullshit."

His nonsense
To me
Makes perfect sense,
And studying you
I understand
—Us.

Better Late Than Never

Your husband
Announces at breakfast—
"Today
Is the first day
Of the rest
Of our lives."

You furrow your brow
And wryly reply—
"I think
You're a week
Late."

Counting Sheep

Like every morning,
I asked my father
About your night;
—How both of you slept?

"We slept great!"
—He cheerfully replied,
Then paused
For comic effect—
"Until three o'clock."

He tells me
He wants a smaller bed;
Less distance to cross,
To pin you down.

You wanted Rody
And your mother.
Pulled the covers.
Cried—
"Help! Help!
We need Help!"
Then segued into—
"Baa, baa, black sheep
Have you any wool?
Yes sir, yes sir,
Three bags full."

Speaking Truth

I appreciate
About you
Your lack
Of deception—
This new
Direct you.

You were mumbling
This morning
And I asked—
"What's that
You're saying mom?"
To which you replied—
"It's all bad."

Having heard
My name
And a word or two,

I knew
You spoke the truth
And knew
I didn't need
—To know.

Is that Your Final Answer?

Is that your final answer?
Is your husband's
Favorite question.

Striking Out

"Hey,
Wait a minute,
How did that pill
Get over there
On the floor?"
Your husband
Wants to know.

You tell him,
You don't know—
"It flew."
He tells you
You need to
Take it;
It's important.
But you inform him—
"I don't like it."

"Oh.
I see."
He laughs—
"Okay.
If you don't like it,
Don't take it."

You tell him
He's being sarcastic.
He tries pleading—
"Will you pleeeez
Take this little pill?"

Your answer—
A resolute
"No."

His final question—
"Is that your final answer?"

Maternal Instinct

I watch you
Every morning
Check on your babies—
Victor and Victoria.

Watch you
Coo and talk
To them;
Entertain them
With *Itsy Bitsy Spider.*

Attentive and warm—
I imagine you
Once upon a time
Checking on
—Me.

Preparation for Life

You taught us
Empathy.
Taught us
To notice;
And to not judge.
Taught us
That those
Hardest to love
Need love
The most.
Taught us
To imagine
Walking
In another's
Shoes.

You prepared me
—For you.

One Day at a Time

There are mornings
And evenings
When you say
Little

—Or nothing
And I wonder
What I will write.

There are
Days
When every word
You speak
Tells a story,
And I wonder
How I will choose
        —Only one.

Yesterday
You provided
A collection,
And I labored
To record
Every nuance
And phrase
—To keep up.

But today's
A new day;
You
—And I—
Have nothing
To say.

Locked In

I laughed
When my father told me
You locked yourself
In Vickie's car.
Another day—
A new adventure.

It wasn't funny
—He didn't laugh.
It took 40 minutes
To set you free.
You were hot
Slumped over
And scared.

My father didn't say
—But I'll say
    He was scared too.
I asked about the
Lesson learned
And he told me
Vickie's plan—
    This was her first time.

He smiled then—
Began to laugh.
"She's done it to me
    Multiple times.
You think I need
A plan too?"

Embrace

I have
Embraced
Your illness.
Embraced
You—
    As you are.
There is
Nothing
Left
Today
I need
Or
Desire
Of you
—Except
    Your embrace.
I wish only
To savor
The pleasure
Of holding
You.

Fulfilling Dreams

You hoped
That one day
I would move
Closer.
You wanted me
In your life—
I wanted
    —My own.

I wish you knew
Our dreams
Came true.

My Double Life

You had a hundred
Questions
For me tonight.
You wanted to know
The name
Of my husband-to-be.
You wanted to know
Who introduced us.
Asked how I knew
He liked me, too.
I tried in vain
To explain
I know
No husband-to-be,
But your questions
Came anyway.
And so it is—
Pregnant in June;
Engaged in November.
I get around!
—And here I thought
I was house bound.

Why Worry?

I sometimes wonder
About my own mind;

Wonder whether
I'm not
Just like you
　　—Minus some time.
But my attention
To detail
Never was
　　What it should be—
Absentminded
As you so readily
Pointed out to me.
So I don't think
I'd mind
Losing my mind;
Living in my own
Reality
　　—Not fully aware.
I might even wager,
I'm already there.

Feeling Neglected

You are our diva
With dementia.
Your every moment
Attended;
Your every mood
Allowed.
From sunrise
To sunset,
Your personal
Entourage
Endeavors
To keep you

Well cared for
And content.
So yes,
I laughed
When yesterday
You thanked me
For paying attention
To you.
Complained—
"No one else does."
And like a child,
Threatening to run away,
Informed me—
*"I am seriously considering
Going to an old folks home."*

Giving Thanks

My father and I
Stayed up talking about
Transformations—
    Our own.
How we are
Neither of us
The same person
    —Thanks to you.
Changed irrevocably.
Centered in contentment
Rich in gratitude
Grounded in love
—Abundantly blessed.

Still Keeping Me Honest

In keeping
With tradition
We sat around
The table
And told tales
    On you—
The psychological trauma
Of our double centennial
Home
And the haunted cellar
Where you made us
    Play.

With dire conviction
And grand theatrics,
I piled torment
On injustice
Until
—You raised your arms
And slowly drew
An imagined bow
Across the strings
Of a phantom violin.
    Silenced
With laughter—
You're still keeping me
Honest.

Peace is Every Step

As we walked
Up the lane
In silence,
I began assembling
Today's poem
In my mind.
A poem about
    Patience
As an ongoing
Practice—
Tested
Stretched
And strengthened
Through
Tears
Meanness
And clenched fists.
    Endurance.
Halfway
To our turning point,
You turned to me
Teary-eyed
Arms open—
"I'm sorry
I was so terrible.
I don't mean to be."

I wrapped you
In my arms
And told you
I understand.
I felt my heart
    Ache—

Stretched
To a new dimension;
Love strengthened.

When your husband
Caught up to us
You told him—
"I'm not scary anymore."

Free Love

Disinclined
To sell
My soul
—A poet
In a profit-driven
World—
I turned
Instead
To prostituting
You.
   One view.
Or could it be
A generosity?
Faith
That love
   Freely given—
Grows.

1. 2. 3.

"MOTHER!"

"Shall we do a Rody?"
"Yeah."

"Okay—
1. 2. 3."
"RODY!"

And this was how
My favorite morning
Began.
The three of us
Lying
In your bed;
The two of you
Practicing
—Yelling.

In the Company of Women

Your husband
Took you on an outing
Today
—Alone.
On the way home
You stopped for lunch.
But you melted down
Between courses,
So he took your lunch
To go

And took you
To the Ladies Room.

He cracked the door
And called in—
"Anybody in there?"
When a voice
Answered
Yes,
You took charge
And marched in.

Your husband waited.

When you emerged
Ten minutes later,
Four ladies
Escorted you.
Your husband
Relating this vignette
Tells me—
"I have no idea
What went on in there."

But I do;
Can easily
Imagine
A community
of women
Loving
Another woman
As if she were
Their mother;
Their aunt
    —Their prayer
For peace.

Eat Play Love

My husband
Painted
   P L A Y
On the walls
Of his office
In large
Colored letters.
He finished
—Then handed me
His wedding ring.

The next day
Angry men
Blew up
New York's Twin Towers
And I undertook
   To understand;
To redefine
   Love.

Your husband's
Voicemail message
Advises callers—
"Put a little love
   And laughter
In all your endeavors;
It will be good for you."

I listened to him
Serenade you
This morning
   His entire repertoire.
You chastised him

For keeping you
Up late last night.
—He feigned surprise.
You told him
It was late
    For you
And he agreed;
6:45 is late.
You told him
"Hold that Tiger"
Is not a love song.
He told you
It is—
To another tiger.

He wiped your lips
So they'd be
"Ready for kissing,"
Then pretended
To steal one.
He asked if all your
Boyfriends
Sing to you?

He coaxed
And cajoled
You
To open your lips
For a smoothie.
Aggravated you.
He asked
If all your boyfriends
Aggravate you?
Then said—
"You know who I am
Don't you?

When that
Smooth-talking
Richard
Comes around,
He wouldn't do that
To you
—No sir.
But that mean, old
Rody
He'd aggravate you."

He tells you he is getting
You ready
For a good day.

Inspired
In the presence
Of so much
Love
    —Innocence
    And laughter—
I am grateful
For this
Hard lesson
Twice learned.
I am grateful
To know
The value of
    PLAY.

1. 2. 3. Redux

Your husband
Left you alone
With me on the iPad
While he went
To the back of the house
To prepare your bed
And brush his teeth.

You fell asleep;
Your head
    Dead weight
Precariously
Pulling you over.

I called
And whistled
For your husband
—To no avail.

I paused
Listening
To the baby monitor
To hear
If he could
Hear
Me.
Instead,
I heard you—
"Why don't we
Try a 1. 2. 3.?"

A brilliant idea!

So we did—
Three
In all.
"1. 2. 3.
R I C H A R D !"

He didn't come
—running—
But alert,
You rose
Your head.
An equally
Effective solution
To an immediate
Need.

Just

Talking about friends
In comparable
Circumstances
You asked—
"What does he have?
Is that better
Or worse —"

"Than what you have?"
—Your husband
Filled in your question
For you.
Then answered,
"You just have
Lewy body dementia
With Parkinson's;

He has Alzheimer's."

You repeated—
"Just."

"Yes,
Just,"
Your husband
Firmly
But gently,
Tells you—
"We're very
Blessed."

Thriving

My father and I
Were talking again
About amazement
　　—Our own.
He recounted
How many
Warnings
He received
About the caregiver's
Toll—
　　"I'm thriving."
I believe him.
I'm thriving, too.

When I'm away
I want to return
To you.
To this absurdity

We share—
This source
Of so much
Love
and laughter.

Does life
Get better
Than this?

Always Thinking

This morning
There was a passionate
Discussion
About the peculiar odor
Emanating
From the floral arrangement
On the kitchen table.
Consensus
Between Vickie
And Richard
Agreed
It smelled
Like cat urine.

I suggested
It might be
The boxwood.
Then added
That boxwood bushes
Make your whole house
Smell.

You,
Seemingly
Not engaged,
Chimed in—
"That would keep him away."

An Inside Job

You hold your crotch
So we ask
If you need to go.
You tell us
You don't
And explain—
*"I don't know
What the story is;
It just gets wet."*

When your husband
Pulls your diaper down
You tell him—
"I didn't do that."

Out and About

It's Saturday
And Vickie-Renee
Plans your day
With you.
She'll take you
To the park
To walk the track
And people watch.

Then by her house
To bake cookies
With her boys.
She knows
You need
A change of scenery
—And so do we.

Say No to Drugs

The other morning
You refused your pills—
One vitamin;
One probiotic.
You pantomimed
Instead
The act
Of smoking.

This morning
You called them
Funny pills.
Defiantly declared—
"I'm not going
To take those—
Not when they're
Funny pills.
I'm not going
To feel funny."

It isn't funny
The pills
They push

To still
Our unwanted.
—If only
You knew.

And the Difference Is?

In a family
Prone
To exaggerate
And fond
of teasing—
        Forgetting
Fits right in.

I tell you
I can't wait
To see you
Tomorrow
And give you
Lots of hugs.
You tell me—
"You haven't
Given me
One of those
        In so long
I can't remember
What it feels like."

Are you teasing?
Or speaking
Your truth?

Everyone laughs.
And the truth
    —If it could be known,
Changes nothing.

Classic

Your husband—
"We're going to have
A good day today."

You—
"Oh dear."

Self Diagnosis

I arrived
At your house
In the afternoon.
Your husband
Pulled three chairs
In front of the wood stove
And we sat by the warmth
And caught up.

I began relating
The story
Of a woman
With advanced
Alzheimer's.
You raised your hand
And I asked—

What is it mom?

"That's probably me."

Your husband
Laughed kindly
And told you—
"Lesley,
You don't even have
Alzheimer's."

But you wanted to know—
*"Well, how come
I'm so dopey?"*

The Mother in Me

Childless
—I imagine
A parent
Feels
Something
Like this—
This way
I feel
At bedtime
When you
Call out
In the dark
And ask me
If I won't stay
With you
A little while.

The way
My heart
Feels
When you
Tell me
You just need
Some cuddling
—And I lie down
Beside you.

Personal Space

You walk into the corner
Of the room
And lean your head
Against the wall—
*"Are you ever
Going to leave me
Alone?"*

You crave
Personal space.
I get this
—I learned
This same need
From you.

Modern Romance

Your husband
Walks into the kitchen
Shaking his head—
"Imagine!
Taking a shower
With someone
And having them ask
   —What's your name?"

Holiday Cheer

At your husband's request,
I wrote your holiday letter
Today;
Here's what you say—

Greetings.

We hope this note finds you and yours healthy and
happy. Our lives are blessed in so many ways that
we are bold in our gratitude. The love that Lesley
and I have received from our community of family
and friends—this year and all our lives—is a
humbling embarrassment of riches.

Our day-to-day is a trial that has taught us to love
our lives fully—in this present moment. To treasure
every day as a sacred gift. Our daughter Page has
captured the journey Lesley and I are sharing by
writing and publishing a poem a day. Ours is a
journey that has guided us out of our heads and
into our hearts. Hearts that have led us together
through this dark passage of uncertainty and
letting go. As we have let go emotionally—and
physically—the children have been helping us de-
clutter and simplify our lives. We have been
buoyed along on a tide of incredible love and joy
for living. Love and laughter lighting our way one
day at a time.

And what you've just read is Page's voice. What I
want to say: Enjoy each day, sunshine or rain, and
put a little love and laughter in all your endeavors.
Willingness to accept fate's burden will lighten the

load in half or more, for fate leads the willing and drags the unwilling. Say today what you might say tomorrow, because tomorrow is so far away.

We love all of you. Thank you for the joy you bring to our lives.

Dick and Lesley

Mind Over Media

It's been years
Since your husband
Turned off the TV.
Our conversations
Censored—
We carefully avoid
Mention
Of everything
And anything
Remotely
Distressing.
No violence;
Talk of money
Politics
Or what we fear.
Even the weather
Gets sanitized;
Natural disasters
And impending storms
Do not get discussed
In front of you.

Only Love
Gratitude
And laughter.

Sensitive
And easily scared,
You
Need it
This way
—And we've learned
    To prefer it.

Delusions and Illusions

We read an article
In the paper—
A woman discussing
Her mother's
Lewy Body Dementia.
She called it
Less common
    And far worse
Than Alzheimer's.
Sited
Her mother's
Hallucinations
As a source
    Of suffering
Greater than
Forgetting.

We call them
    Your spirit people;
Tell you

We're jealous
We can't see
What you do.

A circus
In our front yard—
Elephants
And dancing pigs.
Kids
From another era
Play relay games
While a group of men
Stand around a fire.

Two nights ago
"Whore girls"
Were everywhere,
And there are always
Unattended children
Not properly dressed
For the weather.

You worry
Sometimes
About feeding them.
Get upset
When they chop down
Your trees.
We explain
It's like
Watching TV
—You don't need
To worry
    Just enjoy
    What you see.

Though you require
Reminding,
This works
    — You believe us.

I wonder
Are you
Worse off?
    Are we?
Or is this idea
Of greater
Or less than
Just an illusion?
— Another form
Of delusion.

Calories and Compromise

Each visit
I fill your freezer
With wholesome
Homemade
Soups and stews.
Hearty
Healthy
And easy to eat.
You
Taught me
This
— To choose well
Foods
That would keep me
Well.

We want the same
For you—
And we want
Calories
Too.
So I am
Happy
When I hear
That you ate
    A double!
Cheeseburger
With fries!

For all
Our failed
Efforts
To supersize
Your appetite,
I'm willing to concede
That any meal
—Is a happy meal.

Peace and Goodwill on Christmas Eve

Joy!
To our world
You
Were born.
And through
Your trials
Our hearts
Rejoined.
So let wonders
Never cease

And Heaven
And Nature
Ring
With all this
Joy
We bring
To a world
In need
Of Peace.
May our Truth
Displace
The suffering
And sorrow
Of this holy place—
This planet
So full
Of wonder;
This human race
So capable
Of Grace.

Happy Birthday Mom!

A Merry Day

Your husband
Walked into the room,
   Threw wide his arms
And cheerfully proclaimed—
"Merry Christmas!"

You lit up
Like a holiday tree
And replied—
"It is now."

Sleeping In

At the dinner table
You announced
With pleasure—
"Tomorrow
When I wake up
I can just roll over;
I don't have to get up.
I can sleep in!"

Your husband,
Whom you wake
Every morning
At five
    If not earlier
Laughed
And concurred—
"You do a lot
Of work at night
—All that covers up
And covers down.
That's tiring!"

You looked at him
And smirked—
"You're teasing,
But it's true."

The Art of Conversation

Your voice
Soft
Your language
Muddled
You chat
The whole way
Up the lane
   —And back.

"Hmmm."
"Really?"
"That's interesting."
"Wow!
I didn't know that."
"What do you think?"

I respond
With questions
And remarks
That may
   Or may not
Apply
—But none-the-less
They satisfy.

What it Feels Like

Absorbed in a book,
I felt mildly assaulted
When out of nowhere
You clumsily
Covered my eyes

With your apron
Attempting
To fit it over my head.

"Hey!
Mom,
I don't need an apron"
—I politely objected.

"Well you do it to me."

You're right.

A Happy Coincidence

I hopped out of the car
As your husband
Parked alongside the ATM.
My back turned,
I heard you
Calling me—
*"Kathryn Page
Kathryn Page!"*

I spun around—
"Yes, mom?"

Your husband
Answered—
"We were just parking
And your mom
Saw you—
"Hey, look it's Page!"

He winked at me,
"Can you believe it?
What a coincidence."
And I agreed.

Good Morning

It's a good morning
When we're still able
      To laugh
At life.
My father
Laughed
As he shared
The details
Of his morning
With me.

You wiggled
Most of the way
Out of your diaper
While still in bed,
And as he guided you
Shuffling
To the bathroom
      "Little marbles"
Fell out
All over the floor.

He told me
That without
His glasses on
"They look
Like knotholes

—Only they squish
When you step on them."

We laughed—
Then continued on
With our morning
Routine,
As if this was
     Routine;
Just another day

—And it is.
Another day
We're here to laugh
Along with life—
Lucky
To share so much love.

Year in Review

My father
Reviewed
Your expenses
And shared
His Joy
With me.
He spent
     Six thousand dollars
On your
Pharmaceuticals
In 2011,
     And one hundred dollars
In 2012.

Substituting
Food
For pills
 —A smoothie a day
Kept the doctors
At bay.

Imagine

*"Life's like a movie, write your own ending. Keep
believing, keep pretending."—Jim Henson*

You
Were good friends
With Jim Henson
In college
So we tease
Your husband
That he alone
Is cooler
    Than Kermit.
And in our
Movie
—He and I—
We imagine
Our own ending;
One
Where you
Recover.
    Why not?

There are
Countless
Examples

Of possible—
Things once
Accepted
As not.

Believing
Pretending
Imagining
    —The impossible
Makes more sense
Than expecting
Waiting
Anticipating
Someone else's
    —Inevitable.

Waiting
Without hope
Imagination
Or purpose—
Feels like a stagnant
Oppression.

The UTIs
That plagued you
Have not returned
In over three months.
The phlegm that
Threatened
To choke you—
Abated.
You no longer
Sleep
At the table
Refusing to eat
And each day

We celebrate
Your meals
As monumental
Victories.

Can your mind
Heal?
—Who are we
To say.
So in the meantime,
For our own sake
    And yours
We keep believing.
Keep pretending
And imagining
Our own ending
—The one
In which you
    "Get better and better
    Every day
    In every way"
—Another of your husband's
Favorite things
To say.

His Quest

Like every morning
Your husband finishes
Making and serving
Your smoothie;
Cutting a plate of fresh fruit;
Buttering and warming
A pastry.

He cleans up
And joins you at the table
With his blood pressure cuff.
Delivering variations
Of the same line—
"Good morning,
This is Dr. Nolker.
Have we met before?
Have you been taking
Your pretty pills?"

You interrupt him
This morning—
*"Two things
You made up."*
Your husband
Cracks up.

Perfectly calm
You reply—
*"I'm helping you
Along in your quest."*

"My Quest
Is to follow my Dream
My Lady.
To follow my Dream
To You."

You smile—
"That's right."

Practical Magic

Getting ready for bed
Last evening
You complained
To your husband—
"Santa didn't come.
He didn't even bring one
Christmas tree light!"

Your husband suggested
Maybe you were bad?
But you shot back
    Without hesitation—
"I was perfect!"

You're right
Santa didn't come.
You slept through
Our annual
Recycle exchange;
Missed out
On opening
The packages we wrap
Of the things
We no longer need.

But this morning,
Santa had come.
The kitchen table
Was full of presents
With a note—
"To Lesley
From Santa.
Sorry I'm late."

You ate a big breakfast,
Then opened your gifts
    With tears of overwhelm
—Unable to believe
They were all for you.

New clothes
Your daughter-in-law
Bought you,
Which your husband
Wrapped.

"Old Nick
Really got carried away,
Look at all these nice things"
—Your husband kisses you.

"He did"
—You whisper in agreement.

Then you and Vickie
Head off to your bedroom
To try everything on.

Telepathy

What should we call
This gift
You possess
For reading
Our minds?

I read an article
About men and women
With dementia
Writing poetry.

That evening
You made everything
Rhyme.

Retail Therapy

Who would have
Imagined
You
Would go from death bed
To new clothes
In 90 days?

But here you are
Weighing
90 pounds—
    A record high
Since
Your lull
In the eighties.

You look stylish today
With your skinny legs
In your print leggings
And new sweater
With its Empire cut.

Attractive and practical—
Practically
A new you.

Laughter as Medicine

You made us
Laugh
Uncontrollably—
Outbursts
That continued
To burst out
Long after
The moment
Passed.

You called
Your husband
An old fart.

Tears
Streaming
Down his face,
He asked
What would
His life
Be like
Without you?

"My life
Would be
So dreary!

I haven't laughed
Like that
In weeks,"

He plants a kiss
On your cheek.

You tell us—
"Most people
Never laugh"
—And I wonder
Who is healing
Whom?

Our Harmony

I would rather
Change diapers
Than shop
For you
—Or with you.
So I am grateful
To my sister-in-law
For caring—
And my sister
For carrying
Your old things
Away.
I am grateful
To you
For giving us
This harmony
Of community.

Layers of Letting Go

Cary
Sorted
Cleaned
And bagged
—She stopped counting
    At 45—
Pairs of pants
Ranging
In sizes
From
8–14.
Sweaters
And tops.
Layers
    Of you
—Released
Back into
The stream
Of consumption—
Clothes
For the living.

She called me
For confirmation—
"Do we really
Get rid of everything?"

All that energy
    Released;
A catalog of stories
—Fabric permeated
With the essence
Of emotion.

Threads
That weave
Into the lives
Of others;
The ones who shared
Your moment—
    Remember you
By what you wore.

Decades
Of details
    Discarded
In favor
Of a clean slate
—And this
Simplified
You.

Forgetting to Try

I shook
What felt like
One hundred hands
Yesterday.
Learned
An equally
Daunting
Number of names;
Exchanged intimate details
In meaningful moments
    —None of which
I remember
Today.

At what point
Does inattention
Transition
From laziness
To a diagnosis?

Attagirl

Your husband,
Full of positive
Encouragement,
Gives you another—
"Attagirl"
For eating well.

He asks—
"Are you keeping track
Of all these attagirls
Lesley?"

You nod—
"Umm Hmm.
Good.
Good.
Oops."

A fair
Self-assessment.

Your State of Grace

Do we recognize
The beggar
For our
Teacher?
The State of
Grace
Without a label?
When did
    —You
Become divine?
Which poem
Marks
The crossing
Of that line?

Lessons in Listening

We hear you
Clearly
When you interject
Over the conversation—
"I
Was speaking."

I apologize
And explain
That our video connection
Sometimes lapses;
That I hadn't meant
To cut you off.
I hadn't heard you.

Without opening
Your eyes,
You cut straight
To the truth—
"That can't be so,
You do it
All day long."

Moments later
You demonstrate.
I am speaking
When I hear—
"La, La, La
La, La, La, La,
La, La—
LA, LA, LA, LA."

As I was saying—
Despite your fool's
Facade,
You wisely
Keep us honest.

Your Voice in My Head

When I told
    —Your sister
My intention
To sell
Many
Of my possessions,
She told me—
"Not!
Your good antiques."

Yes,
Mom—
As if
I am not
46.

Her words
Could be
Your words
—Awaken
Dormant memories;
Previous attempts
To give history
The slip.

The voice
Of your conscience
Constant
In my unconscious.

When your sister
Says goodbye,
She tells me
How much
She loves me—
"Even though
You infuriate me!"

I infuriate her
Because she can't
Change me
—That's what
She tells me
Is also why—

"I love you
As much as
I do."

I hang up,
And realize—
That was you,
Too.

Fanfare

First,
Your husband
Praised
Himself—
The success
Of his goose stew.
Then,
Lavishly praised
You.
How you ate
Seconds
—And entertained
Your guests.

"She was talking
Up a storm"—
He brags.

Vickie
Chimes in—
"And her words
Are improving!"

You
Roll your eyes—
*"I could do without
The glory."*

Morning Improv Routine

It was another
One of those
Mornings
When you
Wiggle out
Of your diaper
And wet the bed.

Your husband,
Adopting
The persona
Of a stern Inspector,
Walks over
To your side
And observes—
"I see
Your bed is wet;
And your diaper
Is off."

He asks you
—Still
In character—
"Do you know
Anything
About who
Did this?"

You volley back—
"No!
And I don't care
For you accusing
Me."

The Answer is Love

The answer
According to
Your husband—
    Is Love.

So you ask—
"What's the question?"

Anyway

I'm tired
Tonight
—I don't feel
Like writing
Your poem.
I wasn't
Paying attention
To you
During dinner
—Distracted.

I write
Anyway—
A tribute
To all

The nights
And days
—You
Tired
And distracted—
Showed up
Anyway.

Silent Understanding

Easily
And often
    Enthusiastic
—A lover
Of music—
I like
Volume.
You
    Prefer quiet.
Sensitive
To commotion
And noise,
You are mostly
    Indifferent
To music.

And yet
I discover
I also love
The sound
    Of stillness.
Here,
Where there is only
The hiss

Of the fire;
The baritone gurgles
Of a freezing lake
—And this quiet
understanding
That you and I
Are actually alike.

Weight Watchers

When your weight
Dropped
    In a free fall
From 138
To 83
I wanted
Desperately
To tell
My father
Stop—
—Stop counting
Every pound.

Please don't
Tell me
—The weight
    Of his anguish
Weighing
Heavily
On me.

Nor did I want
My view
Of you

Reduced
To a number;
Hash marks
On a scale
Ticking away
Your time
    Remaining.

But fate
intervened—
    Tipped the scales
In your favor,
And tonight
I ask
—I want to know.

Each decimal
A declaration
    Of possible
—A reason
To tally
Our blessings—
    95
And still counting!

The Beauty of Community

They came tonight
Bearing balloons,
A gourmet meal
And cake.

In years past—
You cooked

And baked;
Set a special table
    And invited them
Your friends
To come
And celebrate
Your husband.

He turns 82
Sunday
And what you
Can no longer do
—They do
    For you.

I marvel
Again
At the beauty
Of community—
As it is meant
To be.
This fellowship
    Of fulfillment.
The potential
    For joy
In even this.

A Hoot without Hooters

Vickie,
Fixing your shirt collar
Commented—
"It's flopping."

To which
You replied—
"He knows
I don't have anything
To flop."

And once again,
We bust out
Laughing.

Undying Desire

Dinner
Winding down,
   Your bedtime
Approaching,
You smile
And tell your husband—
"I look at you
And I think,
Ummm
—I can hardly wait."

The Sound of You

Your snore
Sounds
Like a freight train—
Loud
And guttural.

It begins
The moment
Your eyes close.

In bed,
Asleep on the couch,
—At the table.
A constant
In our lives
—It broadcasts
Over the monitor
Like white noise.

Our rhythmic
Reassurance—
The sound
   Of you
Still breathing.

Your Mind; Your Manners

Manners
Were not
Negotiable—
No elbows
On the table;
Left hand,
Listless
In your lap.
Spine straight,
Head up,
Shoulders back.
No using
Your knife

To corral
Loose peas.
Fork
Switches hands
For cutting
—A single bite
At a time;
Then rests
On your plate
While chewing.

Your fork
Knew
The soft flesh
Of my arm.
And if a quick
Prick
Didn't do the trick,
You threatened us
With the prospect
Of supper
Alone
In the cellar.

So what
Would you say
About your manners
Today?

In the morning,
You threw
Your sweet bun
Across the room
—You'd had enough.

In the evening,
You took
Each bite
Your husband
Proffered
—Didn't care
For what he offered—
Opened up
And spit it out.

What would you say?
Unacceptable!
Of this,
I have no doubt.

Thinking about Stuff

I wonder
At the correlation
Between clutter
    And contentment?
Holding on
    And health?

You held on
    To everything—
Closets
And cabinets;
Dressers
And desks
    Full to overflowing.
The seldom used
And unused
Squirreled away

For a rainy day—
A day
That never came.

I came across
An old photograph
Of you today
     —A much younger woman,
Your hair
Hardly grey,
You are wearing
A pair of pants
I recognize
For having
     Only just
Given away.
And I wonder,
What were you thinking?
—Or if you were?

Positive Spin

You husband raises
Another bite
Of puréed
     —Salad
To your lips,
And with great
Enthusiasm
Declares—
"This is a treat!"

Your salad
Wasn't going down
    Well,
So in a moment
Of improvisation
He threw
    Everything
Into the blender,
With a splash
Of chicken soup.

"Wow!
Am I some cook!
This is delicious!
Don't you agree?"
—He asks.

And unbelievably
—You do.

Too Late to Ask

We all know
Why
Your husband
    Chose you—
Beautiful, smart, kind
Creative
Confident
And independent.

We know the story
    —You
In your green dress

Working at NBC;
Your husband
—Still—
In school.

But I've never stopped
To wonder why—
Why you
      Chose him?
Self-evident,
To my adoring
Eyes—
But today,
I place myself
In your shoes
      Then
And wonder
Why?

Poor
      With a poor reputation
His friends placed bets;
Predicted divorce—
Gave you
      —Six weeks.

You didn't lack
For suitors
—So what about
Him
Suited
You?

I wish I knew.

Trying Times

My father
Affects
A stern tone—

The same one
I remember
Him using
When he scolded
The family dog.

Not terribly
Convincing.

"Lesley!
You stop that
Right now!"

I want to laugh.
But it's not
A laughing
Matter.

It's been months—
I forgot
How you act
With a UTI
—Mean
With a penchant
For hitting;
    Trying.

You begin to cry.
My father patiently

Reasons with you.
Tells you—
"I'm only trying
To help you
Darling;
I love you dearly.
You're getting better,
And I need you
To cooperate.
Your infection
Makes your mind
Strange
And we need
To work together."

He tells you
He doesn't like
To raise his voice.
He reminds you
That you
Don't hit people.
"These are
Trying times
—We must all try
     Harder."

Semantics

Sitting
In front of the fire
Your husband
Runs through
A menu
Of dinner options

And together
You agree on
Lasagna.

At the table
—You refuse
To eat it.
Your husband
Wants to know why?
"I spent all day
Making this;
Aren't you going
To eat it?"

Wise to his ways,
You correct him—
"You did not.
You pulled it out of the freezer."

"But you said
You wanted this"
—He implores.
According to you—
That was yesterday;
He needs
To start paying attention.

He raises a spoonful—
"Try this little bite."
You give him
One of your looks—
"What is it?"

He tells you
Lasagna;
You tell him
No.

"Okay,
How about a bite
Of noodles
With red sauce?"
—That
You agree to eat.

Mean and Ornery

You refuse
Your antibiotic
Each time
You get a UTI.
The first few—
     A battle;
No amount
Of pleading,
Reasoning
—Or running out
Of patience—
Persuades you.

Intractable

At breakfast
Vickie
Succeeded
     Finally
In getting most

Of the contents in
—Mixed in
With something else.

Last night
You won;
Your husband
Gave up.

When he asked you
This morning
Why?
—Why won't you
Take your pill?
You gave him
A perfect,
Clear-headed
reply—
*"Because
I'm mean and ornery."*

Take Two

It's evening,
My father calls me
On FaceTime;
Places the iPad
In front of you.

I say—
"Hello mom!"
You say—
*"Hello
Pagey-Poo."*

I can't remember
The last time
You called me that;
Or knew who
I am
—To you.

I ask
How are you?
And you tell me—
"Better!
My attitude
Is better too."

Great Expectations

Convincing you
That you
Should want
To eat,
Your husband
Reminds you
How well
You've been doing—
"We want
To get you
Up to 100 pounds
Lesley,
Then back
To 130!"
You scrunch
Your face
And cast him
A skeptical look—

"You
Have great expectations."

He laughs
And asks—
"Don't you want
To weigh 130 pounds?"

"No."

Choosing To Live

The trees
Here
Demonstrate
The will
To live—
Tenacious;
Resilient.
Roots
Seek soil
    Where there is none.
—Undaunted
Wrap around
Rocks
And bore
Through
Bedrock.

They
Remind me
Of you.

I hear
My father
Prompt you
This evening
As he guides you
Toward the iPad—
"Say it real loud
So she can hear you."

I wait.
You come into view;
Then announce
Loud and clear—
"HERE I AM."

Indeed!
Like the trees
    Still here
From my childhood
—You choose
To live.

Walking to Wellness

When my father calls
In the evening
You are still asleep—
    Zonked out.
He tells me
He's not sure
Whether there will be
Any dinner.
He came home
In the afternoon

As you and Vickie
Returned
From your
　　Fifth walk!
Up and down
The lane—
Nearly
Two-and-a-half miles
For your
Two toothpicks
To carry you.
He describes
The scene—
You dragging
Like you could
Hardly stand.

Vickie
Tells me
In the morning—
"She was on a roll!
She just kept going."

The will
To be well
And a sunny day—
You are on your way.

The Other One Percent

My father
Carries the paper
To the table
This morning—

"The Wall Street Journal"
He announces—
"Is finally
Catching up
With us;
They're talking
About smoothies.
It's about time!"

He reads out loud
That only
An estimated
    One percent
Of the population
Regularly
Drink smoothies
At home.

Health—
    The true wealth
We all value;
And you,
Vickie,
Your husband
And me—
The one percent.

Our green
Glasses full
—We toast
Our good fortune.

Of One Mind

When you carried me
Inside of you,
You read continuously
    Out loud—
To me.
Then later told me
How you credit
My love of books
And words
To this—
    Shared intimacy
That shaped my destiny.

I think about
That—
Ineffable bond
Between a mother
And her child,
    And of the indivisible bond
Between our emotions
And physiology
—Our psychology.

Perhaps
The mysterious bond
    Of a shared heart
Weakens
With inattention;
Or with intention
—But does it ever
Sever?

My dreams last night
Were full of anxiety
And disquiet;
I woke feeling
Unsettled
And cantankerous.
 —You too
Slept poorly;
Woke in an agitated
State
Of mind.

Our lives intrinsically
 Linked
Right now
—My own awareness
Heightened—
I stop to wonder
If beneath
The surface
We
 You and me
Are not
But two
Expressions
 Of one
Maternal mind;
All feelings
Entwined.

More Discretion Needed

I have been reading
Azar Nafisi's
Memoir
—*Reading Lolita in Tehran*
So I laugh
When you frown
This morning
And out of the blue
Advise me
That I need
To use more caution
—More discretion.

You tell me
That I need
To be
More aware
Of other people.

This familiar
Sentiment—
Your disapproving way
To say
        More like
Other people.

But like Nafisi
And her girls,
I choose to be
        Free
—I love
Being me.

Headed for Paradise

I inquire
About your day
And you
Start talking away.
Most of it
I miss,
Until
I hear—
"And then
We went
To Paradise."

"You went
To Paradise!?"

I tell you
I want to go, too!

Perfectly
Nonchalant,
You tell me
Okay;
Then ask—
"What time
Tomorrow
Would you
Like to go?"

Necessity

My father calls himself
A one-armed paper hanger
Whenever
He's in the kitchen
   —He's frazzled.

His efforts
To get dinner
Prepared
And on the table
   Hampered
By the cat
Howling
For more food;
Me peppering him
With questions
About your day
   —As you
Wander off.

Necessity
The mother of invention,
He solves
His biggest problem
   By tying you
To your chair
With the strings
Of your apron.

I watch
As you attempt
To stand—
   A skill

We're thrilled
You've re-mastered
—But don't necessarily
Want you
To use.

The Power of Attraction

You come to breakfast
"All slicked up"
With your new haircut,
Wearing lipstick
And earrings
—Carrying a bouquet
Of fake violets.

We gush about how
Great!
You look.

Later,
I ask your husband
About his plans
For the day,
And he tells me
Leaning in for a kiss—
"I don't know,
I may just spend
The whole day
Hugging and kissing
Your mom
—She looks so good!"

Listening
To every word,
You say—
"That sounds good to me."

Your husband
Steals
Another kiss—
"Okay,
That's what I'm going to do then."

The Power of Attitude

"I can't stand—"
You stop
Mid-sentence.

Your husband
Fills in—
"You can stand
Anything."

You nod—
*"Anybody can do anything
They have to do."*

Blah, Blah, Blah, Blah

*"What!
Are you carrying on
About?!"*

You interrupt
Your husband's
    Daily
Dinner
    Sales routine;
His motivational
Banter
Intended
To encourage you
To eat
    Even more.

You look
At me—
"I don't know
If you hear him,
But he just goes
Blah, Blah, Blah, Blah."

Stay in Bed Day

No one
Is coming in
To help
This weekend,
And when
I still hadn't heard
From your husband
At a quarter past
    Nine,
I called
To confirm

Everything
Is fine.

You are both
   Still in bed,
Heads
Under the covers—
   Hiding.

You
—From a room crowded
With hallucinations;
Your husband—
From the specter
Of a day
Filled to capacity
With caring
For you.

If he has his way—
You might
Stay in bed
All day.

Funny Valentine

You told your husband
When you first married—
"If you can't think
Of anything more creative
Than a heart-shaped box
Of chocolates
For Valentine's
   —Don't bother."

Every year,
    For fifty-seven
Your husband
Has selected the tackiest
Heart-shaped box
Of chocolates
That he can find.
—He's your funny valentine.

Perspective

Dinner is cooking;
You are sleeping
And my father and I
Are discussing
    Perspective.

There are so many
Markers
We monitor—
    Sleeping
    Eating
    Walking
    Talking
    Crying
    Voiding.

"Perspective."
Your husband
Chuckles—
"A good day
Is when your wife
Has a nice bowel movement.

—I never thought about
    That
When we were dating in college."

He begins
To really laugh—
"A GREAT day
Is when your wife
Has a nice bowel movement
—And Vickie's here!"

We proceed to remember
Your memorable—
    Movements.
The one you partially wrapped
In toilet paper
    Then handed
To your husband
Outside the ladies room
In Walmart.

The standing
Poops
    In the living room.
The mega millions;
The power ball—
Your lottery draw.

Both of us laughing,
My father says to me—
"Who would have thought
Dementia
    Could be so much fun."

Perspective indeed
—It's what we all need.

Your Beautiful Response

"Good morning Mom.
Don't you look pretty
This morning."

I am not expecting
Your response;
But after years
Of working
    On myself
I am unfazed
When you say—
"Yes.
Don't you wish you
Could look like this."

No mom,
I silently reply
—I am happy
I look
Like me.

If the Shoe Fits

It is not
Necessarily
So
That if the shoe
Fits
You should
Wear it
—But you do.

First,
Your husband
Discovered
Stones
    Large ones
In your sneaker
—You'd walked
All day
Without complaint.

On a different occasion,
Sitting by the fire,
He noticed
You wearing
Your shoes
    On the wrong feet
—His doing
    Which hadn't occurred
    To you
To ask him
To undo.

Of Two Minds

There is no point
To worrying—
You taught me this
While modeling
    Worry.

I think about
Your duality
    And my own
Tonight

As I wait for my father
To call.
Always punctual
    He's very late;
He's not answering
Either phone.

Of two minds
    My own debate.
Each side supplying
Compelling
—Conjecture.

You are both sound asleep;
Or, something's gone wrong
—With you.

You have plans
You forgot to mention;
Or, something's gone wrong
—With your husband.

And so the two
Continue to debate
While patiently
I wait.
And when you do
Call
The answer
—Not one
I considered
At all.

Trading Places

I greet you
—Good morning
And you ask
If I'd like to trade places
    With you.

"You want me
To trade places
With you?"
—I confirm.

You tell me—
"For a little while."

Is this
For empathy's sake?
Or because
You need a break?

Maiden, Mother, Crone

I spent the weekend
With Cary
Whose unconditional
    Love
Carried me through
My difficult days
When your love
Felt
    —Conditional.

Her love
Sustains me
Still.

Older
Than I am
I counted
On her
—Maternal
Nature—
When you and I
Could not
See
Eye to eye.

You loved us
Equally
—Related to us
    Differently.
And absent
Any jealousy,
We make our own—
Sacred trinity.

Angels Among Us

Some days
I feel like an old woman;
My old man,
Another child
Grown old.

We sat around the table
And sang—

Angel from Montgomery
The night before
My friends' child
   —Was born.

This river of life
A constant flow
Of death
   And rebirth:
—Our own identities;
Our loved ones.

We pray
For one thing
That we can hold onto,
   To believe in this living
—Such a hard row
To hoe.

But there are
Angels
   Among us—
Disguised
As you
And me.

I tell Vickie
This morning
How my father
Tells me—
"Everyone thinks
That Vickie's a normal person,
But she's not—
She's an angel
Sent to take care of me."

Listening,
You add—
"And me."

Love
To hold onto;
A reason
To believe.

Torn to Pieces

We can be torn
To pieces
By circumstance
—Or be
    Amused
And choose
To play along.

Your husband
Compliments
You this evening—
His tone
A balance struck
Between teasing
    And acceptance.

"You're doing a fine job
At tearing up that napkin
Lesley,
Would you like another one?
I've got one here;
You can start fresh."

Oblivious
To the jest,
You accept his offer
—Begin to tear
His napkin too.

No Hurry

Distracted
　　By everything
All of which is
　　Nothing;
Breakfast
Drags on
And on.

Your husband
Nonchalantly
Suggests—
"If we hurry a little
Lesley,
We can maybe
Be finished with this
—By lunch time."

Clowning Around

When I was born,
My brother and sister
Told you
Not to sing—
To me.

Told you
You sang
Off key.

They'd been
Teased at school
And didn't want
That happening
To me.

Today
I wonder
What we missed
When I hear you
Sing along
To your husband's
Favorite song—

"Have I told you lately
That I love you;
Have I told you lately
That I care."

His song ends
But you don't stop
Adding your own—
*"Bee bop bee bop
Dee bop."*

We laugh
And you inform us—
*"Not everything
Is tired
And run down."*

I wish you had
Sang
—Had always
Been a clown.

Pushing Buttons

You gave us
Your catatonic treatment
Last night.
Dinner—
By your husband's
Own admission,
Lacked any redeeming
Qualities
And you wanted
    Nothing
To do with it
—Or us.

Your husband
Cheerfully
Bantered away—
"Here you go,
Open up.
You do open up
Don't you?
Come on,
Open wide.
I've got a delicious bite
Right here.
Does your opening
Mechanism work?"

I mostly watched;
Occasionally
Chimed in
        —To no avail.
Then feeling ornery,
Suggested that I knew
How to get a reaction
Out of you
—I'd found
Your button
Last week,
And guessed correctly
It would work
        Again.

"Mom,"
I began—
"You need to eat
To give your body
strength—"

But before I even
Finished
You snapped
To attention—
"Jesus Page!
Knock it off!"

Then promptly
Returned
To playing
Mute.

Emotional

I wrote an essay
About our experience
And read it out loud
To your husband.
    I waited
For a response
—Unable
To see
His expression—
    Unaware
I'd made him
Cry.

He doesn't read
My poems
    For this reason.

"I guess
Because I'm living this
It makes me emotional
To hear it
—Summed up."

He apologizes.

"Dad,"
I tell him,
"It is emotional—
I think I make a lot of people
Cry."

He laughs,
Breaking the tension—

"In that case,
You should be
Ashamed of yourself
—Making people
Cry."

Cha-Cha

The rhumba
And the cancan
—Your husband
Dances you
From one room
To the next.
From the fire
To the table;
The bedroom
To the kitchen.
Mixing up styles,
He dances
To keep you
Focused
—To keep you
Moving.

Special

Why
Do we fear
And reject
What we simultaneously
Call
—Special?

Isn't it
The heart's
Greatest desire
To feel
—Needed?

Those
With special
Needs
    Need us
The most,
And yet
We label them
—Unfortunate.

Fortunately—
The Vickies
Know how
To embrace
    Your special
    Needs
Blessed as well
With their own
Special
Love.

Spoken Like a Modern Woman

At breakfast
You asked the group—
*"Does everybody
Have a partner?"*

Your husband answered—
"I sure do!
I have a beautiful partner."

He asked you then
If you do?
And when you answered
No,
He wanted to know
If you'd like one?

You wanted to know—
"Do I have to clean up
After him?"

Live Strong

As Vickie
Lowered you
Onto the toilet seat
You told her—
"I'm scared."

She told you—
"I'm strong."

You told her—
"I'm not."

Then you told
Your husband
You want to exercise

—You want
Strong arms.

He got out
Your 5 pound weights
And you lift
    Our spirits
When you ask
To lift them.

Tears of Joy

Tonight
When your husband
Asks why you're crying,
You tell him—
*"Because
I'm so happy."*

He tells you,
He's happy too.

You Could Have Danced All Night

When your husband
Helps you stand up
From the dinner table,
He asks you
If you'd care to dance.

You shake your hips,
Wiggle down low
And kick your legs.

When the song ends,
You tell him
You want to keep dancing.

Three songs later,
You smile and whisper—
"That was really fun!"

The Caregiver's Eight Step Path

We were told
    —Forewarned
About the caregiver's
Toll.
But Niki Henderson
Had already
Told me
About being
With the breakdown
    —Until you breakthrough.
Inspired me.

Seven steps
To a state
    Of Grace—
I counted them
This morning.

Empathy
Forgiveness;
Acceptance
And surrender.
Presence—
Which yields

Joy
—Catalyzes
Magic
That delivers you
To a state of Grace.

This state
Of so much
    Love
—And laughter.
This path
    Of joy and fulfillment
Available
To anyone—
    Willing
To break down.

Niki Henderson, Executive Director of People's Grocery, spoke at the 2013 Business Alliance of Living Local Economies (BALLE) conference, held in Buffalo, NY.

Non-Attachment

After acceptance
    Of what is
Comes surrender
    To not knowing.

Your husband
Left you alone
    For only a moment
Dressed
In the bathroom
Brushing your teeth.

You fell.

You hit your head.

This vulnerability
    Of not knowing
Makes the certainty
    Of this moment
—A gift.

Free
Of judgment
And full
From loving you,
I indulge
Shamelessly
In the richness
    Of right now
And feel
Abundantly
    —Fulfilled.

Alone

The iPad
Went down
Sometime
During the day
Yesterday
    After your fall
—But unlike
You

The iPad
Didn't fare well.

I ate dinner
Alone.

I Woke up
This morning
Alone.

Same Problem; Different Day

You
And the garage door
Share a common problem.
The door
Won't close
All the way
—Not quite
To the floor.
You won't
Open your mouth
All the way
—Not quite
Wide enough
To fit in a fork.

Every day
Your husband
"Fixes"
The door;
And every morning
It stops working
—Again.

He doesn't seem
To mind.
Nor does he mind
That every evening
He spends the meal
Reminding you
How to open wide.

Too Tired to Talk

My father called
And we each
Gave a brief
Update
Of our day.

I'm exhausted
From packing
My house.
Your husband
Claims to be
Exhausted
From baking
Fresh bread
And an apple pie.

You usually
Doze
This time of day;
Before dinner
Sitting
In front of the fire.

Tonight,
We all napped
    —No conversation,
Just a virtual chorus
Of snores.

A Nice Domestic Scene

Every evening
When my father calls
He asks—
"Would you like to see
A nice domestic scene?"

Every evening
He shows me
    You
Sitting in an armchair
With a fat, black cat
Curled
    And content
In your arms.

Every Day in Every Way

You're getting
Better
    And better
Every day
    In every way
—Another of your husband's
Favorite things to say.
Just maybe—

It's true,
For you
Tipped the scales today.
You weigh 100 pounds!
A benchmark
That simply astounds!
Confounds
Convention
—Precisely
Our intention.

To Live is a Choice

To live
—Is a choice.
Graffiti
Painted
On my kitchen wall.

Sleeping,
I dream
Repeatedly
About dying—
    And not
—Dying.

Lucid,
I note
My calm indifference
To the prospect
Of leaving
—And the same
passive detachment
    To staying.

An impersonal
Acceptance
Without
Preference—
One path
Neither better
Or worse
Than the other.

And I wonder
When I wake,
At your will
    To stay
—What life force
Compels you
To struggle?
To choose
Living
When dying
Feels
—So natural.

Babies, Teenagers and You

You've been
Sleeping
    A lot
Lately
—Long naps
And
Long nights.
Is your body
Shutting down?

Or
Working hard?

They look
The same.

Fine Line

I
Rearrange
My things
—And what
I do
Is called
 Decorating.
You
Rearrange
Your things
—And what
You do
Is called
 Dementia.
When I
Rearranged
My things
As a child
—What I did
Was called
 Obsessive
 Compulsive.

When I
Rearrange
My things
Today—

I call
My compositions
    Art.

Adult Education

Your husband
Confirms
That the water glasses
Should be
Placed above the knives
—Then expresses
Pleasure
At mastering
Another domestic detail.

Laundry
Shopping
Cooking;
Your constant care
And supervision.
House affairs
And social obligations.

Like a gender reassignment;
Because of you
—His life is new.

Waking Up is Hard to Do

You no longer
Cry
And act anxious
During the day
—But every morning
You wake
In tears
Talking to
And about
People
    We can't see.
Disoriented
And disturbed—
Your transition
Troubles you.

Double Vision

To forgive you
—I needed
To see you.

In seeing you—
I saw myself.

Mrs. America

There were
No tears
This morning
—You were animated
And full of yourself.

Vickie
Helped you dress,
And when you entered
The kitchen
Where your husband
   Waited,
He made his usual
Fuss—
"Don't you look
Beautiful!
Wow-wee!!
Here she comes"
He breaks into song—
"Miss America!"

You strut
   In slow motion
Wiggle your hips
And confidently
Inform him—
"It's Mrs.
Mrs. America."

Your husband
Kisses you
—And you pretend
To tremble.

On the Go

I still remember
The day
I took away
    Your right
To drive.
As the only one
Who rode with you
—Instead of
Drove for you—
Only I knew.

There was no
Diagnosis
    Yet;
Only my
"Say-so"
Which you
Challenged—
"What do you know!"

Friends came
And got you;
Your husband
Chauffeured you.
Nothing changed—
    Your point of view.
You called it jail;
And me—
Your jailer.

You never cared
To be on the go

Until
You couldn't
Be—
Spontaneous.

Now,
The first thing
You want to know
When you see
Vickie—
"Where are we going?"
And off you go!

Expand. Contract.

I didn't write
Yesterday.
Happy and clear
The day before
—Moving forward.
Overwhelmed
And breaking down
The next.

You
Amazed us all
On Wednesday—
You heard Vickie
Talking to her partner
On the speakerphone
While driving
—And from the backseat
Crystal clear
And loud

Chimed in—
"Hello Gary.
Stay warm
And be safe."

This morning
You fell
Again;
You're fine
Again
—And so am I.

Good days
And bad days—
Like all of
Nature,
We expand
    And contract
In harmony
With our unfolding
Lives.

Obstinate

Your husband
Asks you
If you'd like
A piece of grapefruit.
You emphatically
Tell him—
"No."
"I thought you like
Grapefruit?"
—He asks.

You answer
That you do;
    You love it!
Confused,
He says—
"I'm fixing this grapefruit
For you."
You give him a look
And reply—
"Well, I'm not eating it
—I can tell you that."
He smiles
And wants to know
If you are familiar
With the word—
    Obstinate.
You tilt your head
Thinking
And ask—
"Should I be?"

Rody Never Gets in Trouble

You never fuss
    At Rody
—Jackie
Or Mary.
But Richard
And Page—
You remember
Our names
    Without fail
Whenever you're
Vexed.

Helpless

You
Have another
UTI.
—I
Hate
The helplessness
I feel
Watching
Your husband
Beg you
To take
Your medicine.
Your troubled
Mind
Tells you
To refuse;
Every time.

Dressing is a Slow Process

Negotiating
Your thin limbs
Into sleeves
And leggings
Is never
What you might call
Easy.
Frail
And unsteady
—Tugging
And pulling

While
Propping
And holding
   Is an art
All its own.

You rarely
Help;
You usually
Hinder.
Grabbing hold
Of sleeves
And necklines
   Or our clothes
Your grip
Is ironclad
And generally
—Non-negotiable.

Happy to See Me

You and Vickie
Greeted us
In the lane
Today
—Out walking
When I arrived.

Your husband
Rolled down
The window
And said—

"Look who's here
Lesley,
—I've got
Page the Rage
With me."

Your face
Changed
From smiling
    To crying.
Reminding me
Of all my visits
Growing up
—How you always
    Cried
When I arrived—
And never
When I left.

Who is Lord Pumpernickel?

You wanted
To go
To the bathroom
—But wouldn't
Allow me
To lower your pants.
Told me—
"No!"
In no
Uncertain
—And the most
Uncommon—
Terms.

Told me—
"I don't care
If you're going to see
Lord Pumpernickel!
You are not
Pulling them down!"
At that
I couldn't stop
Laughing
—Even you
Laughed, too.

Childlike

On this day
Of rebirth
And innocence
I finally
Appreciate
    The child
In you.

Not the one
That takes
Two hours
To feed.
Or the child
Who throws
Tantrums
And pummels me
With feather-light
Fists.

Today
I embraced
    The child
In you
Who lights up
At the sight
Of an Easter basket
The Easter bunny
Left
—Especially for you.

Food Games

Feeding you
Has become
A competitive
    Game.

Your husband
And I
Flank you
At the table,
Each of us
With forks
Poised
—Waiting.
Persuading.
Laughing.

You say—
"Umm hmm,"
When we ask
If you're ready;

If you'd like
A bite
Of this
Or that
Well garnished
—With adjectives
Of enticement.

Umm hmm
Is better than
No
—Though it is
No
Guarantee.

Between
Pursed lips
And wide open
    Is the partial open
—A slim opportunity
For heaping
Forkfuls.

Forcing food
In with fingers
Counts
—Food that
Goes in
And
Comes out
    Does not.

The real skill
Is patience
—Results
Are pure luck.

Fishing for Solutions

Fishing
For a winner
—I prepared
A gourmet dinner.
To avoid the risk
Of rejection—
I puréed
    Everything
To perfection.
You ate
Twice as much
At double
Your speed.
Reassessing
Conditions
—Smooth
Is the new need.

The Mirror Doesn't Lie

Mirror
Mirror
On the wall
Who is
That woman
Bent
And small?
You stare
Into mirrors
Transfixed
By your
Reflection

And I ache
For you
When I wonder
How it feels.
Feeble
And frail
With droopy
Eyes,
You listen
To our lavish
Praise—
And call it
Lies.

Ladies of Leisure

I read
That boredom
Is one of the
Worst
Attributes
Of dementia.

In the beginning,
That was true
For you—
    And us
Who tried
In vain
To find activities
That you
Could do.

Now every day
You eat
Breakfast
And are on your way
—You and Vickie
Running errands
And visiting parks.
You browse
The stores,
Watch horses run
And children
Play—
    Stay out all day.

The Magic Bullet

We found
Your magic bullet—
It's called
The Nutribullet.
Purée
Is passé
—We've stepped
    Into liquid.
There is no
Thinking
Involved
In drinking—
No confusion
About
The meaning of
    —Open
No troublesome chewing.

The only trouble
Now,
As your husband
Pointed out—
What will I
Write about?

Dementia Detective Agent Page Nolker

I feel like
A detective—
Noting circumstances
Considering clues
Alert to every
Subtle shift
In you.

Are you worse
Because
You fell
Last week
—Without
A witness—
And maybe hit
Your head?

Or is it
The medicine
Your husband
Administers
To you
Just before
Bed?

Confused
By labels
—He bought
The wrong kind
Containing
Narcotics
That mess with
Your mind.

Or is it
More simple
Than any of that?
Just the ebb
And flow
—The way
Things must go.

Calm and Collected

Your brain struggles
With fundamental
Motor skills
Like spitting
And swallowing—
Yet somehow
You found the will
—Still knew
What to do.
Choking in bed
Face red
Eyes scared
—You could not
    Breathe.
And yet—

You knew
To ring the bells
Placed next to you.

Frantic
And frightened
—Alone
Together—
I heaved you up
And bent you over
—Pulled mucus
From your mouth
 And begged you
To cough;
To spit—
 To understand.

And when the moment
 Passed—
—Your breath
Congested
But no longer
 Arrested—
I imposed
A peace in me
 For you
But you
Were already calm
—Comforting
 Me.
How could that
Be?

Grandma? Is that You?

I answered your phone
And was asked—
"Grandma?
Is that you?"

Wise to the guise
I played along—
"Why yes,
It is.
Hello."

"Do you know
Who this is?
Can you hear me?"
—Came his query.

"I can
And I do;
How are you?"

    Do I sound
    Like a grandma?!
    I wanted to say,
    But instead
    I continued to play.

A willing decoy
I waited to hear
What scam
He'd employ.
They call your number
    Without your name—

Pretend to know you
Just the same.

Your credit card
The IRS
"Customer service"
—Without an address.
They trade on fear
And doubt—
Are bold
—You're singled out
For being old.

The Bright Side of This Dark Disease

The discord
Of dementia
    Became
This harmony
Of family
Embracing
—Endless days
The sum of moments
Mercurial—
    Turned into
    Treasured days
The sum of moments
Memorable:
Docile
Feisty
Frustrated
Sweet
Confused
Inconsolable

Tired
Agitated
Asleep
Busy
Still
Busy
Anxious
Distracted
Afraid
Delusional
Sarcastic
Stubborn
Incoherent
Innocent
Funny
Churlish—
Cherished.
One year
Later,
You're more
Or less
The same,
While we
Remain
Forever—
Changed.

It's a Wonderful World

Compassionate
Expressions
    Form lasting impressions.
Andrea
At Walmart

Remembered you—
Despite not
Seeing you
In a year
Or two.
Fondly greeted us
    With an open heart,
And shared
How glad she felt
To see
The two of you—
Still managing
    Okay.
Recalled the day
She helped
Your husband
    By helping you—
Use the loo.
A compassionate act
For a stranger
To do.

Rolling

Merrily
We roll along.
Over dinner
We celebrated
Being on a roll
    —Riding high!
Amazed
To see you
Eat
More in one meal

Than you ate
In a week.
By bedtime
We'd detected
That your foot
Was infected—
Replacing
Our cheer
Came a wave
Of fresh
    Fear.
That crisis
Resolved
—Without doctors
Involved—
We emerged from
The dip
Better equipped.
Yes,
Merrily
We roll along
    —Up
Then down
    And up again—
Happy
With hope
And able
To cope.

What Would I Do?

Your husband
Is sick
—In bed
Fighting a cold
In his chest
And his head.
He doesn't need
Administering to,
But it has me
Wondering
What I would do
If I had to care
For the two
Of you?

The Bad Side of Good

With every action
    A reaction.
Unfortunate
Side effects
That coincide
With the good side
Of our best
—Intentions.
Progress
Unmade
Where results
Are made.
Well-fed
You go to bed.
You sleep

All night—
    At last
We're doing
Something right.
But when you wake
—There's our
Mistake—
You're sopping wet
To our regret.
For all we try—
We've caused another
UTI.

Without Regret

I was sorry
To read
That a literary
Luminary
I love
Felt the need
To live with regret.
At 84—
I expected
More.
I thought she
Should know
That wrong
    More than right
Is what gives us
Clear sight.
That to know
What it means
To forgive

—We must first
Be willing
To live.

Love is Not a Pie

I watched
A Korean comedy
With your husband
Last night.
We were still
Laughing
This morning—
It wouldn't have been
Your thing.

But he and I
Have always shared
    A love
For similar things—
Philosophy and history
Life's mysteries
And comedies.
You'd feel
Left out;
    Complain
You felt
Ignored
When I came home.

I made you
Jealous.
I didn't mean to;
    I didn't want to—

I didn't know what to do.
A source
Of distress
I could never
Address.
Love is not
    A pie—
Enjoying more
Doesn't leave you
—With less.

You and I
Shared different
Joys;
You and he—
A private love
That has nothing
To do
—With me.

How I wanted
You
To see
You had no reason
To be
Jealous
Of me.
I hope you
Know that
Now;
Know how
He loves—
    All of life
—Especially
You,
His wife.

Now or Not Yet?

Caught between
States of consciousness
   —Transitioning
From sleeping
To waking—
You open
Your eyes
   Wide
And talk to us
While still
   Snoring loudly.

Do we get you up?
Or allow you
   To lapse
Back to sleep?
We must decide.

Will your death
   Feel liminal?
Force us
To choose
Between
Now—
Or
Not yet?

Tied Up

We knot
Your apron strings
To the back

Of the kitchen chair
—Not entirely
Fair.
This isn't
To keep you
In place—
It's to keep you
From bunching
Your apron
Up to your face.
I forget
These ties
When I suggest
You rise.
You struggle
In your chair
     You try
Until at last
I realize.

What Do Elephant Trainer's Do?

Terrified
Of falling
You will not
—Lift
Your foot
For me.
You're holding
On
—I'm holding
You—
Will not fall
But still

You balk.
I'm down on
My knees
—Begging you
Please.
You will not
Shift
Though I try to lift
—Your foot
And though
You do not
Weigh
A thing
—I feel like
An elephant
Trainer
In the ring.

Cutting to the Chase

A good friend
Dropped by
To visit.
You chatted
A bit
Then cut
To the chase
And chased
Him away.
"Bill,
We love you
Dearly"
—You said
Loud and clearly—

"But we'll love you
Better—
When you leave."

Leading Questions

Your husband
Does not enjoy
Brushing your teeth
  —Neither do I.
From the bedroom
I hear him ask—
"Lesley,
Would you like
Page
To brush your teeth
Tonight?"

He calls to me
—Informing me
I've been requested.

I inform him—
Leading questions
Don't count.

"Mom,"
I ask—
"Would you like Dad
To brush your teeth
Tonight?"

You reply
That you would.

He should
Know better
Than misleading
Me.

Fishy

Sick today,
I asked
For your husband's
Help;
Assigned him
The marinade.
Not waiting
For me to explain,
He pulled out
The notecard
I'd made
With everything
He needed
To know.
But when dinner
Came,
My condition
The same,
I shuffled through
The kitchen
To let him know—
"I'm headed to bed."

Panic!
With a grin
He stuttered
And stammered

Protested—
"But what do I do
With that fish!?"
I rolled my eyes—
"Do what you do
When I'm not around."
I walked through
The steps,
Including the blending—
Fish
Leftover squash
And ice cubes of stock.

"Stock ice cubes?!
Where do I
Find those?"
—He demanded to know.

My favorite
    Wise man
Playing
His favorite role
—The incompetent fool.

Just Another Day

The skin doctor
Called
With your biopsy
Results—
    Cancer
In three places.

So we'll
Scrape them
Off
—And carry
On.

The Empathy of Experience

Sore
Nauseous
Feverish
And tired
—Of feeling
Sore
Nauseous
Feverish
And tired.
    My health
Will eventually
Improve—
    Yours
Will not.

Will it Feel Like This?

Will it feel like this
    When you're gone?
I gaze at you
From across the room
—As close
As I dare come.
My heart fills
With love

And this visceral longing
    To touch you.
To bridge
Our communication gap
Through the language
We both understand
—My fingers
Scratching your head.
My hands holding yours.
Caressing your cheeks;
    Lips kissing your temples.
Will I feel like this
    When you're gone?
So full of love
And unfulfilled too.

Heart and Mind

I lose touch
With the present
When I cannot
    Touch you.
Without
A physical anchor
For my
Presence
—My mind
Drifts.
It wanders
In the direction
It believes
Is home—
Gets lost
In the details

Of things
Left undone.
None of which
Matter
    To a heart
Which feels
At home
Wherever
Love lives.

Ready But Not Waiting

I no longer wonder
When I leave
    If it's the last time
I'll hold you.

I've learned
To love you
    Like it is
And continue
Living
    Like it isn't.

Ready
—But not waiting.

No Hard Feelings

They say
People with dementia
Prefer
The familiarity

Of home—
You
Can't wait
To climb into
Vickie's car
Every morning
    And leave.
When the day
Is over
You cry
—You're never
Ready
To come home.

Disappearing by Degrees

Your husband
Still calls me
In the morning
But I do not see you
Before we hang up.
I hear you
In the background
Over the baby monitor
    —Snoring;
But I will not see you
Until evening.
When I do
    You will be napping
In the chair
While he fixes your dinner.
At the table
He'll place the iPad
In front of you

Then hold a glass
To your lips
    For the duration
Of the meal—
    Precluding
Conversation.
When you finish
—We'll say goodnight
And I'll wonder
    Did you know
I was there?

Exhausted

I want to tell the truth
—To tell your husband
When he asks
That I am
    Exhausted—
Overwhelmed.
But my list
Of petty complaints
Seem selfish
And insubstantial
Compared
To those
He could offer—
    But never does.
Instead
He tells me
    Matter-of-factly
How the first doctor
You saw this morning
Found

That you suffer
From allergies;
And the second
Scraped away
　　Your cancer.
He tells me
That your walk
This evening
　　Tired you out
And you were unable
To make it up
The four steps
Into the house.
　　He lifted
　　Your dead weight
　　Into his arms
And carried you
　　—Which tired him.
He tells me
That the
"Lottery drawing"
He won this afternoon
Was—
　　"Beyond belief!"
All this
He tells me
With his indefatigable
　　Good nature
And I know
That his exhaustion
Runs deep

Beneath his placid surface
—A current he cannot
Afford

To acknowledge
Until your dying day.

No Response

You fix Vickie
    With a look
And say—
"You ask as many
Questions
As that other lady."

I am
    The other lady.
I ask questions
Without hope
Of answers
Only to fill
The air space
Between us.
So now
    Instead
I ramble on
Sharing details
    About nothing
And expecting
    Nothing
In response.
I tell you
There's a breeze
Out of the east
And it may
    Or may not
Rain.

I tell you
There are new people
    Living
On our lane,
But we haven't met
Yet.
I tell you
What I did with my day
And you stare at me
In that same
    Disinterested way.

Another Mother's Day

The first time
    I miscarried
It was my birthday;
The last time
    Was mother's day.
If I were
A mother, too
—Would it ease the pain
Of losing you?

A Web of Care

The same community
That cares about you
Cares about me
    —And needs care, too.
Your friends
Are older;

My love
And concern
Does not stop
With you.

Respite

I need
A respite
From carrying
This care
—A break
For my own
Mental health's
Sake.
My writing
Will resume
When my energy
Renews.

Change

You changed
Overnight
    —In the stroke
Of a moment.

I struggle
To adjust
To our new
    Reality
Helpless

—And longing
To touch you.
To hug my father.

You sit in your chair
    Moaning
Coughing
Choking;
    Tears
Run down your cheeks.
You cannot swallow;
    Dinner
Runs down your chin.

Patient
Loving
    Always positive
—My father
Remains
Unchanged.

Rage

Anger—
The last emotion
I dreamt of feeling
    Now
In this moment
Of Grace.
I confirmed with Vickie,
Checked in
With my siblings
And sent your husband
With you

To the doctor
Yesterday
  —Before the weekend
  Arrives.
The doctor needs
To approve you
For the auspices
Of hospice.
We want to keep you
Comfortable
  And let you go.
We do not want
A medical end
  —Only relief from pain;
We've made
Our desire clear.

What lies
Between his ears
That he can't hear?
He said
You just needed
  More time
In hospital care
—You'd be back
  To "baseline."

Whose baseline?
  And why?
He insisted on
Admitting you—
So your husband and you
Spent ten hours
In ER—
  Uncomfortable and scared.
And in the end,

Were told
The doctor
    Was wrong—
You don't have pneumonia;
You have dementia
—And it has progressed.

Yes—
They confirmed,
Bring your wife home
And make her
    Comfortable.
—Only now
We have to wait
Through the weekend
To make
    Comfortable
Possible.

Peaceful

This is the peaceful
Potential
I prayed for
—And dreamt of.

My sister
Showered and dressed you;
Together we carried you
To your chair.
You have not woken
Through all of it.
Nor have you
Coughed

Or moaned
—Only snored quietly.
The day is beautiful—
The windows open;
A light breeze
Filters through the room.
Quintessential Eastern Shore
—The reason
You chose this home—
    This life.

Your husband's band
Played a gig
By the water
Today—
    Music
    Sailboats
    And friends
—His kind of day.
He kneels beside you now
And softly sings—
"Have I told you lately
That I love you?"

He asks—
"Darling,
Would you like to wake up?"
Then answers—
"No,
I guess you wouldn't."

He kisses you—
"You're a sweetheart
If there ever was one;
We've made a good pair."

You continue
To quietly snore
—There is nothing more
To do
But carry on
With loving you.

Gathering

I prayed
That you would wake
And share a moment
Of recognition
With your son
And his family
When they arrived
—As you had shared
With my sister
And me.
Would know
We gathered
Together in love.

When they arrived
Your husband decided
To try again
    To feed you.
It had been
Two
Days
Since your last meal.
Miraculously—
You woke

And drank
Two
Smoothies.

From the table
Where we gathered
Sharing dinner
—Love and laughter—
I watched you.
You began to move
And mumble
—To try and rise.
Alert—
Your intention clear.
We brought you
To the table,
Where you
Completed
Our circle of Love.

The Roller Coaster

You rallied
Yesterday
—Eyes open
Talking
    Lucid.
Still too much
Tongue
To understand
    But conscious
Enough
To comprehend.
I scratched your head;

I read;
You ate—
    We wait.
Today
You snore
But nothing more.

Hospice

Our fears
Relieved
—Into the sheltering arms
Of Hospice
We were received.

Amazing Grace
And dignity
—Humanity
As it was meant
To be.

Family Ties

What are these
Invisible ties
That bind us
    One to another?
The mathematics
Of life
—Patterns
Choreographed

Into a mysterious
Weave?

My college reunion
This weekend
Reminds me
      That your mother
Died
My graduation day.
      Your sister
Taken ill
—Suddenly
And unexpectedly—
Died
Yesterday.

What are these
Invisible ties
That bind us
      One to another?
The mathematics
Of life
—Patterns
Choreographed
Into a mysterious
Weave?

Comfort Companions

They say
Animals
      Know.
Your cat
And my dog

Alternate shifts
Your constant
    Companions
They lie down
Beside you.
Grateful
—I find comfort
In believing
They comfort
You.

The Circle of Life

As you lay
Dying
A turtle
Came today
To the backdoor
Searching
For a safe place
To lay
Her eggs.

Have I Told You Lately That I Love You

My sister and I
Crawled into bed
With your husband
As soon as
We woke;
One of us
On each side.

He told us
About the songbird
Outside his window
This morning
—How it sang
The same song
    The first verse
Repeatedly.

He told us
How eventually
It was all
He could hear.

I asked—
"Was it pretty?"

"No"
—He laughed,
"It sounded
A lot like—"
And he began
To sing
The same refrain
He sang
    Repeatedly
For you
Straight through—
"Have I told you lately
That I love you."

My mother passed swiftly and peacefully yesterday morning, in her bed, with my father, Vickie and me around her—holding her; telling her we love her. It was a beautiful day to die, and all things considered, a beautiful way.

Whispering Wind

The leaves
Whisper
With the wind
And I hear
    You
Whisper
Too—
"Love
Just gets
Bigger."

" And in the end
    these things matter most
How well did you love?
How fully did you live?
How deeply did you let go?"
    —Jack Kornfield

Afterword

My mother died June 8, 2015. That same month, my father and I came to the lake house to grieve and heal together. In July, my dog died. In September, my father received a pacemaker; by January, a diagnosis of mesothelioma. Opting to forgo traditional medicine, together we studied nutrition, energy medicine and alternative healing—as we continued our practice of love and laughter. On August 25th, 2016, my father died at home in his armchair, surrounded by his three children. But that's another love story for another book.

Acknowledgments

This book is also dedicated to Vickie and Vickie, the two angels who cared for my mother as if she was their own. Through their love and support, they made this story possible.

To my family—for the deep respect and harmony we share with one another.

To the creative muses who helped me make *Materials on Hand* a reality: Anita, Brooke, Laura and Marlaina.

And lastly, I remain incredibly grateful to the friends and strangers on Facebook who travelled this leg of our journey with us. Their messages of love and gratitude helped more than they'll ever know.

Who Am I?

I am a poet
Modeling
Love
Conquering
Fear
In the circumstances
We dread
Which are always
　　—Near.
Unconditional
Love
Dissolving
Conditioned
Responses;
The Art
Of being more
Than the sum
Of All
We fear.

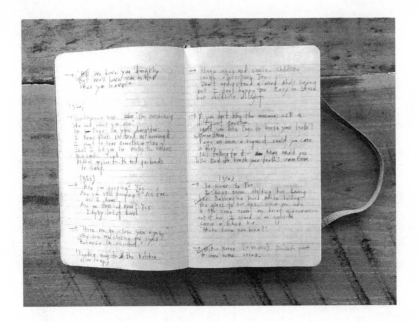

The stories that came before this one, and the stories that come after, can all be found at BabeEffect.com.

I invite you to join me there.

63402538R00215

Made in the USA
Middletown, DE
01 February 2018